"Amy Orr-Ewing has given a tremendous gift to every woman who has longed for a mentor. In these pages, you will find letters that come with love and wisdom. You will know that you are not alone and that the God who made you has called you to lead. I pray this book provokes the rise of a new generation of female leaders in all spheres of life—for the glory of God and for the good of the world."

—**Glenn Packiam**, lead pastor, Rockharbor Church; author, *The Resilient Pastor*; coauthor, *The Intentional Year*

"Amy's book is a pearl of wisdom, soaked with the honest, practical realities of a life spent pursuing Jesus. She speaks as a lover of truth, in kind authority, with bold freedom. I want to read and reread this book and give a copy to every young leader I know. I'm grateful that Amy lives all that she has written in these pages, modeling the authentic intimacy of one who has spent her life saying 'yes' to Jesus. Her example invites me to follow Jesus more bravely and beautifully."

—**Canon Sarah Yardley**, mission lead, Creation Fest UK

"Amy Orr-Ewing has written another book that every female Christ follower must read. In each of her letters we find invaluable, practical information about leading—from fighting anxiety when speaking to navigating work and calling. Amy does not shy away from the more controversial questions, such as whether women should teach in the church. I needed to read every page in this book. Thank you, Amy."

—**Rev. Lisa Wink Schultz**, Chief of Staff, US Senate Chaplain

T0191050

"Amy's letter-writing style provides women with digestible key lessons for leading in the church, in the family, and in the workplace—or in all three. After beginning with gentle letters of encouragement, she leads readers to the hardest and perhaps most important lessons: how to respond to others, care for them, and heal when a Christian organization's leadership has been harmful, deceitful, and abusive. The wisest of men will seek out this book as well."

—**Elizabeth Berridge**, Baroness Berridge of the Vale of Catmose

"Intelligent but heartfelt, sophisticated yet raw, *Lead Like the Real You* hits every key theme in modern female leadership right on the head. This book courageously digs deep into each issue commonly faced by women leaders, including the tabooed and glossed-over ones. This is a manual for every faithful female pioneer who wishes not just to survive but to flourish in the workplace and in life."

—**Ilaria Chan**, chairwoman, Tech for Good Institute

Lead Like the Real You

Previous Books by Amy Orr-Ewing

*Mary's Voice: Advent Reflections to Contemplate
the Coming of Christ*

Where Is God in All the Suffering?

Why Trust the Bible? Answers to Ten Tough Questions

Lead Like the Real You

the

Real You

WISDOM FOR WOMEN ON FINDING
YOUR VOICE, PURSUING GOD'S CALLING,
AND LEADING WITH COURAGE

AMY ORR-EWING

BrazosPress

a division of Baker Publishing Group
Grand Rapids, Michigan

© 2024 by Amy Orr-Ewing

Published by Brazos Press
a division of Baker Publishing Group
Grand Rapids, Michigan
BrazosPress.com

Printed in the United States of America

Library of Congress Cataloging-in-Publication Data
Names: Orr-Ewing, Amy, author.
Title: Lead like the real you : wisdom for women on finding your voice, pursuing God's calling, and leading with courage / Amy Orr-Ewing.
Description: Grand Rapids, Michigan : Brazos Press, a division of Baker Publishing Group, [2024] | Includes bibliographical references.
Identifiers: LCCN 2023056279 | ISBN 9781587436062 (paperback) | ISBN 9781587436376 (casebound) | ISBN 9781493446452 (ebook)
Subjects: LCSH: Christian leadership. | Leadership in women. | Christian women.
Classification: LCC BV652.1 .O57 2024 | DDC 253.082—dc23/eng/20240126
LC record available at https://lccn.loc.gov/2023056279

Cover design by Kathleen Lynch / Black Kat Design

The author is represented by Punchline Agency, LLC.

Baker Publishing Group publications use paper produced from sustainable forestry practices and postconsumer waste whenever possible.

24   25   26   27   28   29   30   7   6   5   4   3   2   1

In loving memory of my oma,

Elisabeth Kopsch
(1913–96),
a woman whose love and courage shaped my life

Contents

Preface

What do I wish I, as a leader, could have known without learning the hard way? That is the burning question that lies at the heart of this book.

Lead Like the Real You is aimed at women who want to grow in leadership wherever God has placed them. Christian women in churches, ministries, and other professional spaces often lack mentors and do not have forerunners in leadership they can look to because so few have gone ahead of them. I hope the pages that follow address this need by way of deeply personal and practical letters aimed at helping Christian women grow in faith and leadership within their context.

The themes addressed in this book are varied and include learning to use your voice, work and calling, facing chauvinism in Christian spaces, pursuing leadership success, addressing abuse and injustice, finding hope in dark times, and navigating friendship—among others. I write with a desire to combine deep connection to Scripture with a grasp of the cultural moment in which we live.

For the past three decades, I have been leading in the church, in theology, and in presenting the Christian faith; traveling the world as a speaker and raising up teams. I have faced opposition for being a woman, navigated an abuse crisis with a celebrity Christian leader, grappled with the big apologetic questions of the day, and ministered to many people who long for mentorship and encouragement in the practical challenges that life throws our way. I have found that wisdom and resilience in leadership and life are virtues we need to fight for; they don't come about by accident. We also need support to grow, and that can be difficult to access.

I have had the opportunity to work with leaders in political, commercial, academic, creative, and church-based settings in nearly forty countries. I have met outstanding women who have inspired me with their tenacity, courage, creativity, and resilience. But the genuine challenges and questions facing women who lead also resonate with me. Our need for companionship on this journey is real. And so I began to write letters of encouragement and advice to Jo—a young leader I first came across as she was graduating university, a woman who reminded me very much of myself at that age. These letters became something more. They were written to Jo and her generation, but as I began to reflect on my own life, I saw they were also written with compassion and hope for the young woman I once was.

Leadership can be a painful and lonely road. I pray that as you read each letter that follows you will know that many women of my age and stage are rooting for you. I hope that as you read of my own personal experiences and struggles you will draw strength, wisdom, and courage for your journey.

PART 1

Learning to Use Your Voice

Proclamation

Dear Jo,

I am sitting in a café in London near St. Mary Woolnoth, where John Newton spent the last years of his life preaching. From here he influenced William Wilberforce, Charles Simeon, Hannah More, and many others. I am writing today because I want to share with you something that I think is really important for your growth as a leader and for this rising generation of Christians. It's the power of words and, for the Christian specifically, the power of proclamation.

It has become fashionable in some circles to quote the famous words attributed to St. Francis of Assisi: "Preach the gospel at all times. When necessary, use words." But we see throughout the New Testament and from early church history onward that words have always been indispensable. Words are powerful. We need the ministry of proclamation—we need to hear the Word of God preached with fire. And whether or not you are called to evangelize or even to speak in public, you are called to *proclaim*.

It has never been more urgent to redress the disillusionment with preaching. Abuses of the gift have meant that we have grown weary and suspicious. But I am praying for a displacing of this ennui with a resurgent hunger for the fire and light of Christ coming to us through the preached Word. "Proclamation," said D. Martyn Lloyd-Jones, is "theology coming through a man who is on fire."[1] I think he should have included women, but the point stands.

Dietrich Bonhoeffer, the German pastor and theologian killed by Hitler's regime, speaks of the living encounter with Jesus through preaching. It is "not a medium of expression for something else, something that lies behind it, but rather it is Christ himself, walking through his congregation as the Word."[2] That is something to hunger for and to experience regularly—Christ the living Word walking through his congregation. Don't give up on proclamation, both hearing it and doing it.

There are more speeches in the book of Acts than in many other historical books of the era, such as the writings of Thucidydes and Heroditus. According to one scholar, this is because Luke, the author of Acts, "is chronicling a historical movement that was carried forward, in the main, by evangelistic preaching. This distinguished his work from that of other historians who are more interested in the macro historical events involving wars, political manoevurings and the like."[3] The early Christians knew that the power of God was closely connected to proclamation.

The Acts of the Apostles records the *process* by which the message of Jesus advances through the whole world. Core elements of this are proclamation of the gospel, miraculous signs, and care for the poor.

Proclamation of the truth matters. Don't lose heart over this. Don't let the charlatans, celebrities, or profiteers rob you of enjoying this gift, whether you serve by using it or receive by regularly listening to it. In my own life and leadership, both disciplines of serving and listening have proven crucial. I am called to step up and proclaim truth with courage and boldness in a context where many have no faith, with hope in the face of despair where it is easy to lose heart. I also know that I need to listen to the preached Word as a regular disciple, that this is an integral part of how I grow as a Christian in the community of faith.

May you find strength and courage as you consistently proclaim the Word or listen to the Word proclaimed. Rediscover the joy of proclamation.

With love,
Amy

Speaking in Public

Dear Jo,

As I prepare to speak to women working in European Union policymaking, I feel prompted to write to you about handling nerves. If you have ever spoken in public or gone through intense examination, you will be familiar with the feeling of dread followed by adrenaline pumping through your body. This is something you are going to need to learn to manage in a healthy way. I have found a few things really help.

First, be prepared. As a woman speaker, whether in a ministry, academic, or corporate setting, I have found preparation to be crucial to offering an original, meaningful, and thoroughly thought-through message. Prepare excellent content that you feel needs to be shared, but also think about how people learn and grasp things best. A coherent structure matters, but humor and memorable illustrations are also essential.

Practice giving your message. Studies show that people decide very quickly, in the first thirty seconds of a speech, whether they like the speaker, are prepared to trust what is being said, and will engage with the presentation.[1] So during those crucial opening lines when you need to connect with your listeners, you are at your most vulnerable. I suggest memorizing your opening lines. Think about your body language. Start with a confident, open body stance with eyes up and a friendly facial expression. People find this reassuring, and it also helps your voice settle.

Second, in the immediate build-up to speaking, when the dread and fear are rumbling, go outside if you can. Walk or run and pray. Take in the natural surroundings and name your physical sensations to God. God has made you in a body. Breathe in and out deeply and slowly. As you speak and own your feelings, invite God into them. Doing so helps you remember that you are not alone in your calling. It also means you aren't denying, repressing, or avoiding reality.

Third, in the few moments before starting, let the adrenaline come. Don't fight it or fear it. God has created you to be able to speak publicly. He is calling you to speak in this moment for your job or to proclaim his Word in a ministry context. Invite the Holy Spirit to fill and empower you. Go for it. If you get the opportunity to speak in a gospel context, "Preach the word; be prepared in season and out of season" (2 Tim. 4:2).

Fourth, after you have finished speaking, you may have an ongoing surge of energy. You may feel elated. This is often followed by a bit of a crash. Be ready for both. Give both to God. Find a healthy pattern with food that works for you. Personally, I can't eat at all before speaking or immediately afterward. But at some point, I need food, especially if I've prayed for a lot of people and I need to drive home. Pay attention to that physical need.

You matter to God. He cares for you. In whatever context you are speaking publicly, you can grow. But I want to share for a moment about preaching in particular. God calls people to be preachers—not machines. And he calls women as well as men. Let him tend to you before, during, and after preaching.

Don't use a preaching gift for gratification, seeking praise and adulation from people, or the rush of a performance and a responsive crowd. That path leads to manipulation and an unhealthy performance orientation. Equally, be careful not to get burned out or beaten up through carrying this gift. It is a weight to carry, and the exertion of doing it well can be crushing if too many demands are placed on the psyche and body of one person. I would also caution you to guard against carrying a responsibility to "deliver" a certain outcome; the hopes and expectations of those organizing an event or bringing others to hear you is a burden that is God's to carry, not yours. Prepare diligently and give the burden of the rest of it to Jesus in prayer.

I have preached in nearly forty countries over more than twenty-five years; I pray I will be able to keep going until I die. I pray the same for you—this precious gift of proclamation is so needed in our generation. There is a famine of the Word of the Lord. But the gift is also precarious—it can be dangerous in the wrong hands, used for harm, control, manipulation, and self-aggrandizement. So be careful, be humble, be intentional, and be kind. Let the Lord tend to you, and be wise in the way you steward the gift. I hope you keep going.

With love,
Amy

Owning Our Embodied Voices

Dear Jo,

For many years, part of my work has involved theological training in various contexts, raising up evangelists and speakers all over the world, many of whom are women. What a privilege! Far more than with male speakers, one of the questions asked by women is "What does my voice sound like?"

Studies show that sounds in the higher register are more likely to annoy or irritate listeners than sounds in the lower register.[1] When we are nervous, our voices often go higher in pitch and we speak more rapidly. In the crucial opening sentences of a sermon or speech, these tendencies can make it more difficult for us to connect with listeners.

A few deep breaths, a conscious effort to keep nerves under control and to slow down our pace, and some practice holding your voice at its natural register without letting it go higher are helpful. But time and again it has struck me that so few women have had the training and support that could help them find their voice. At least this one barrier to women speakers connecting well can certainly be overcome with practical help.

A woman who is confident and secure in her God-given voice is a powerful thing to behold. And her voice is embodied, not theoretical. Her voice is designed to be heard by others. But it will often be heard alongside her image, which is seen either in person or on screen. When we speak, our words are heard, but our bodies are also communicating nonverbally. Posture, stance, mannerisms, and facial expressions matter. Without becoming overly self-conscious, watch a video of yourself speaking and then practice controlling the distracting ticks or mannerisms you notice. Ask a trusted friend for honest feedback. Think about how your body is speaking and what you are hoping to communicate. Good starting points are confidence in God, safety for the listener, commitment to the message, and integrity of life and heart.

Unfortunately for women, clothes also matter. I don't know any men who speak and expect to receive comments about their clothing. I don't know any women who speak and don't expect to receive comments about what they wore. I have found that I need specific speaking outfits that do not distract (patterns can cause issues for cameras), don't show sweat, are comfortable to move in, don't crease on the way, and are modest by reasonable standards. The outfit I wear needs to show respect for the organizers and the listeners. I need to be neither underdressed in corporate, political, or some conference settings nor overdressed in youth, church planting, or other conference settings. I always take heeled shoes along with me, as most lecterns are too high for me without them.

Finding the right thing to wear can feel like a mission, so once you have found it you may wear it over and over again. A warning from personal experience is that I did this too much with one blazer, showing up at an event on Capitol Hill wearing the same blazer I had worn at the White House ten years earlier. Then I wore the same blazer eight years later to an event in Parliament. My husband found the photographs. On the upside, I reminded him how worried I had been to spend $120 on the blazer at the time.

Parallel to the challenges of owning our embodied voices is the pressure to compete or compare ourselves with other women. Don't do that. Jesus has given you your voice with its unique tone and all the twists and turns of your life's journey that make it unique. Resist the temptation to adopt someone else's voice. There is no one "feminine" voice. The Scriptures introduce us to different kinds of godly women, whether young or old, who used their voices. Deborah was called to national, political, and spiritual leadership with a voice that matched. Lydia, a successful business-woman, used her voice to become a house church leader in Philippi. Miriam led God's people in song and dance. Ruth used her voice to overcome intense poverty and suffering and build relationships that would influence the birth line of the Messiah. Phoebe led the Roman church, exercising extraordinary influence over many, including Paul himself.

Your voice is precious, unique, embodied. Find it, steward it, and use it.

With very much love,
Amy

Don't Hold Back

Dear Jo,

I am writing to you from the theology faculty library at the University of Oxford. Silence is mandatory here, so all you can hear is the creak of the odd chair and the tapping of fingers on keyboards. The silence has me asking what happens when women stay quiet—not just in the library but in leadership settings too.

Have you noticed that whenever your influence grows—you take on a new position, start a new ministry, or gain readers and followers online—something internal holds you back from speaking up? Are you aware of that voice in your head holding you back, questioning your ability and perhaps even your right to be in the room?

Whether it's speaking in a leadership meeting, asking a question, or contributing thoughts in a public forum, many women struggle much more than men do to find and use their voice and influence.

This is not just in our heads. Despite all our advances in equality, evidence suggests that women are less likely than men to speak up in professional and educational settings. At university, women are two and a half times less likely than men to ask a question in an academic department seminar. And this is true at every stage of our academic careers. Even senior women ask fewer questions in public settings than men, and women are far less likely to speak up if the first person to ask a question is a man.[1]

Given these facts regarding academic and professional settings, it's not a surprise that we face the same reality in ministry. I recall trying to explain this a few years ago to a national church leader in the

United Kingdom. He has long been egalitarian, and we have worked together at conferences and on projects. He found it unfathomable that I felt any reluctance to speak up or ask a question. His perception of my confident persona in various leadership settings did not compute with what he now heard me saying. It felt like a hugely vulnerable step to share my experience with him. And if competent, accomplished, and experienced women leaders feel this hesitancy, it is likely that some of the emerging female leaders we seek to raise up feel it all the more. We are responsible for creating contexts in which women are safe to speak up and free to contribute their insights.

A number of years ago, the late queen Elizabeth II hosted a reception at Buckingham Palace for women who had made a significant contribution to public life. People from various career paths—fashion designers, athletes, scientists, judges, politicians, musicians, authors, charity entrepreneurs, and academics—attended.

A writer who was there wrote an article about the event. It struck this writer that, in a palace reception room filled with leaders in their field, who were invited by the queen, every person the writer quoted began the conversation saying, "Well, I don't know why I am here . . ." This may just be classic British self-deprecation, but the writer felt it would be inconceivable that a male in an equivalent gathering would have uttered that phrase.

Common thoughts occurring to women in positions of influence when they are about to use their voices include:

Don't be too pushy.
Who am I to say this?
Others here have something more important to contribute than I do. I should let them.
Am I absolutely certain I have my facts right?

It takes real courage to press through the onslaught of self-doubt and speak up. But when you do, two things happen. First, you contribute, fulfilling the purpose for which you are there in the first place. Second, you model something for other women, showing them it is safe for them to fully play their part.

Almost three decades into my working life, I find I still need to work at this. When I am at an academic conference where I know my qualifications and work experience are equal to those of my peers, I still worry about making a point lest I don't have my facts quite right or my thoughts completely distilled. I still need to exercise courage and overcome my fear. At gatherings with leaders who are friends and peers in ministry, I know the organizers want me to share what I think. But a reluctance bubbles up, as there are many nuances at play. I am conscious of the need to have my content clear and correct, but I am also navigating the dynamics of difference. I am aware that I will be speaking as a woman, with all that entails. I must avoid being too pushy or seeming to want to attract the wrong kind of attention. I must show that I am competent in the subject matter without flaunting my learning or experience. So many dynamics are involved in avoiding the negative gender stereotypes associated with the space I am in. All this is a lot to weigh before making a spontaneous statement.

I write this to you because when I was younger I thought these feelings would pass when I became established in my field and could count myself more qualified and more experienced. But they have not completely gone away. So you may as well begin today. Choose today to stop second-guessing yourself and enter fully the opportunities you have. Doing so is not unfeminine or pushy. Jesus commended women who involved themselves, who stepped up and showed up, like the woman with the flow of blood who reached out and grabbed his garment in faith so that power went out from him and healed her (Luke 8:43–48), or the Gentile woman who persisted in asking Jesus to heal her demon-possessed daughter (Mark 7:25–30). When Mary took up a position previously reserved for men and sat at the feet of Jesus to be taught, her sister, Martha, objected and asked that she be put back to work in a stereotypically feminine domestic role. But Jesus commended Mary, saying that she has "chosen what is better, and it *will not be taken away from her*" (Luke 10:42, emphasis added).

If you feel something is holding you back from speaking up and you find yourself questioning your ability and perhaps even your right to be in the room, you are not alone. But maybe it's time to remember Jesus's encouragement to women. Jesus, whose crucifixion and resurrection were witnessed primarily by women. Jesus, whose ministry was financially supported by women and who called women his disciples. Jesus, who entrusted one of the greatest doctrinal statements of the New Testament to a woman when he told Martha, "I am the resurrection and the life" (John 11:25), ensuring that subsequent generations get to read it in the Bible. Jesus, who inspired a woman to be the first evangelist in John's Gospel when he met her at a well in Samaria. Jesus forthrightly and intentionally called, inspired, and anointed women to play specific key roles of *public* witness.

So when the impulse to hold back and second-guess yourself strikes, why not ask Jesus for the courage to break through and for his help in finding and stewarding your voice in all he has called you to? Don't stay quiet; trust him and speak up.

With very much love,
Amy

PART 2

Work and Calling

Calling Unfolds

Dear Jo,

People often ask me, "How did you end up doing what you do?" and "How do you know what God is calling you to do?"

I could not have pictured what I have ended up doing as there was no woman I knew of whose work looked anything like my current work. It is hard to visualize something you don't see elsewhere. But in my experience, this doesn't have to be a negative thing. I have come to realize that a calling dawns on us slowly rather than being mapped out neatly in advance. It can be unhelpful to give each other the impression that we have always had everything all worked out.

I had dreams of mission and ministry as a teenager, but as a woman I did not see a pathway to such things. At university, I began being asked to give short talks and evangelistic messages. This was a complementarian setting—guided by the belief that leadership and teaching positions in the church should be held exclusively by men—so my speaking there involved breaking some unwritten rules. I slowly realized that although there were sporadic opportunities to lead small groups and even to present publicly to larger audiences, there was no pathway or training suitable for me. As I prayed about what work I would do after earning my degree, I realized that I loved speaking and that I seemed to lean toward offering evidence for the gospel. I don't think I knew the word *apologetics* yet other than as something that happened in the first century of the early church.

At this stage, I could imagine two careers that would support a love of evidence and evangelism: a lawyer or an academic. I prayed for direction, but nothing spectacular happened, so I decided to apply for a graduate training contract in a London law firm that would pay for law school and to see at the same time whether the option of academia would be open to me. After a rigorous round of interviews, I was surprised to be offered the training contract.

In prayer, I continued to set these two pathways—the law and academia—before God. I prayed that if he wanted me to follow the academic route, he would make that clear. The clear sign I would need for academia would be getting what is known as a "first-class degree" in the UK (which entails ranking among the top handful of students), since this would open the way to doctoral studies and funding options. At that time, this was a very remote possibility at Oxford, where I was studying.

I felt a high level of peace about law school until I received a phone call from Oxford three days before our final results were due to be published. I was being summoned for a *viva voce*—an oral examination. I was to appear before fourteen dons (senior professors) and answer their questions before my degree grade could be confirmed. This had not happened to an undergraduate in theology for at least twenty years and was scheduled for the day before my wedding.[1]

I lived to tell the tale and was awarded the first-class degree. This seemed like the clear sign in favor of an academic career I had asked God for, and while I did not know it at the time, the experience also served to prepare me for the many question-and-answer sessions I would go on to encounter in my speaking ministry around the world.

This is what prayer and discernment looked like for me: looking at real options, taking practical steps, and praying at each point for guidance.

Calling unfolds in life. We do not often see the path stretching far ahead of us. We need to take each step in faithfulness, praying about the small decisions as well as the larger ones. God often guides us through the relationships we form, our preferences and abilities, the opportunities that arise for us, and our experiences. Even seemingly insignificant decisions can often turn out, in hindsight, to matter. Every step forward for me—from speaking in political settings, to leading missions in universities, to having the opportunity to publish books—emerged in the context of a friendship or the kindness of a leader who I didn't know well but who saw my work and offered me the opportunity to step into something new.

In retrospect, one's calling may look as if it were all mapped out and completely clear, but in my experience, God's leading happens in small-scale increments, through faithfulness and the kindness of friends and colleagues. I encourage you not to over-think your career path or to expect a clear road map. Be faithful in each stage and opportunity—however small. Work hard to get the qualifications you need and the apprenticeships or jobs that match your gifts, preferences, and skills. Let God open doors of opportunity for you. Seek him and be open to his prompting. He asks us to be faithful in little so that he may trust us with much.

With love,
Amy

God Calls Work Good

Dear Jo,

As I travel into the financial district of London today to speak at an investment bank, I am writing to you from the train. I am giving thanks for the Christians who work in these spaces. There can be an unhealthy tendency among Christians to think of "Christian work" as superior to "secular work." I have met so many people who feel disappointed that God didn't call them to full-time ministry, and this feeling largely comes down to their beliefs about what work is.

At the same time, the broader cultural narrative about work subjects us to another pressure. Does the work I do provide significant financial benefit to me, and does it confer a level of status on me according to cultural values? Is my work respectable and profitable? Those in full-time Christian ministry will often answer no to those questions. Whether we feel we are missing out because we are doing "secular work" or because we are in "Christian work," most of us will at some point have feelings of inadequacy.

I believe this uncertainty about the value of our work is a profound question of our age, because it strikes at the heart of human purpose and identity. On a practical level, our work is what we will spend a very large number of waking hours doing. It really matters. Scripture speaks to the ache within each of us, wherever we find ourselves, with regard to our work.

Genesis 1:27 states that the first man and woman were made in the image of God. In that chapter, the primary revelation of God is as Creator, and so we see woven into the earliest account of what it means to be human this idea of creative work. The theological implication of this is that all human work begins primarily in the creative rather than the economic sphere. Humanity created in the image of a creative God images God by working and creating. From a biblical perspective, a common misconception about work is that it is a result of the fall. But even before the fall, Genesis envisages work not merely as utilitarian or even economic but as glorious creativity outworking a divine pattern.

It is of course true that the first Adam was cursed with labor and suffering: "through painful toil you will eat" (Gen. 3:17). The difficulty and economic necessity of work were new and ominous things resulting from sin. Work must now pay. Viewing a person and their work through an economic lens is part of the curse of the first Adam. When Jesus comes as the second Adam, hope and redemption come on many levels. One of those levels is human vocation. Our work can be redeemed, and our sense of purpose and creative potential and vision can be set free from the reductive lens of money and profit.

A biblical perspective on work calls for a whole new way of thinking so that work is not merely something people have to endure to make money but something that can be humane, creative, and life-giving. This means we approach work not with the question "How much does it pay?" but with the question "Is the work good, beautiful, and true?" We can look at a worker and ask not "How much do they earn?" but "What is the worth of their work—does it have integrity, coherence, dignity, and creative or beneficial use?"[1]

This sounds highly impracticable and perhaps even naive. But the work of our hands, minds, and bodies needs to be considered at a much deeper level than merely the economic. Work is a moral question, a matter of human value and divine image. And it sits within our mandate to steward God's creation well, meaning that the environmental impact of our work matters.

Can we begin to work in such a way that we honor the image of God in other human beings, steward well the creation God has entrusted to us, reflect the image of a Creator God, and reject the need to pursue consumption and status?

Our work might also be a means of worship—if we pursue quality, beauty, truth, and integrity in what we make, write, and build. Dorothy Sayers writes, "Work is not, primarily, a thing one does to live, but the thing one lives to do. It is, or it should be, the full expression of the worker's faculties, the thing in which he finds spiritual, mental and bodily satisfaction, and the medium in which he offers himself to God."[2] We can live out our Christian calling in our work by being authentic and truthful in our dealings with others.

All this means you are not a "lesser" Christian if you work outside a church or ministry context. Far from it. You are living out the creation mandate of Genesis to reflect the Creator in whose image we are made. And if the work you spend your time and labor on does not pay much, or anything at all, your value and the value of your work are not reduced. This includes charitable, domestic, or mothering work. The true value of your work lies in its relationship to the Creator you reflect. Does your work carry the integrity, truth, beauty, and authenticity of God? Is your work coherent, true, loving, beneficial, creative, just, or good? These are the questions that should concern us and that will lead to healthy stewardship of the natural world entrusted to us and will point to the redemptive power of the second Adam, Jesus Christ, as a beacon of hope.

Don't lose heart, and may God free you from an oppressive or reductive vision of work.

With love,
Amy

Parenting and Work

Dear Jo,

Even if you are not a parent yourself, the teams you lead are likely to include women who are considering questions about balancing work and childcare. This is a discourse that impacts women of all ages.

Not all of us will become parents, but one of the issues that arises in the discussions around leading and raising children is what we believe work is. If work is viewed primarily through an economic, utilitarian, production-oriented lens, then only work that pays or produces measurable financial benefit has value. But as I shared in letter 6, the Bible doesn't envision work this way. The two most significant themes in a redemptive view of work are stewardship and creativity. As God's image bearers, we have been given a mandate to steward God's creation with the work of our hands. This kind of work is a gift to humanity from a loving God given before the fall. And as human beings made in the image of God, we reflect his nature as Creator by being creative ourselves. God engages in two kinds of creation in Genesis 1 and 2. Creation from nothing, *bara'*, means "bringing into existence" and is used to describe only what God does (see Gen. 1:1, 21, 27; 2:3, 4), and *'asah* involves a rearranging of matter into the varied and beautiful world around us (see Gen. 1:7, 16, 25, 31). When we work, we engage in this *'asah* kind of creativity.

For many women, their relationship with work is fraught with complexity. In the Western world during the 1950s, there was a push in society for women not to "work" so that jobs were available for men returning from the Second World War. Within the church, this became conflated with a theology that limited women to the domestic sphere to focus on child-rearing and housekeeping. A woman who worked outside the home alongside raising children was seen as inferior or suspect.

Outside the church from the 1980s onward, there has been a push for women to be treated equally in the workplace and to be economically productive. Women who choose to stay at home and raise their children are seen as inferior.

Both positions are to be resisted if we have a biblical view of stewardship and creativity. But in many Christian communities, they are in tension. If work and calling are not primarily economic matters, then all women are working. This is true whether a woman serves in ministry, writes books, leads in a corporate setting, designs buildings, cuts hair, serves on the board of a company or charity, or raises children. A woman may or may not receive financial recompense for her work, but regardless of this, the value of her work stands. All the unpaid work we do in raising children, caring for elderly parents, or serving our community through sports clubs, homeless shelters, or school associations has value.

Resist the impetus to feel guilt for spending too much or too little time raising children, and focus instead on finding a God-given rhythm of work in the season of life you are in. Children are a gift to you, your family, and your community. Find a pattern that dignifies them with love, care, attachment, education, and connection. Steward the time you have with children well. Be present. Pay attention to them. Show them the value of work, and liberate them from viewing work as solely economic. But take care that they also see women operating in spheres outside the purely domestic. Show them that human life reflects the creativity of the one in whose image we are made.

Your work has value far greater than money. Work has value in and of itself. By working with integrity, you are reflecting the image of the Creator and fulfilling his mandate to be a steward of this earth.

If you are wrestling with questions of vocation and parenthood, you are not alone. I have learned to approach work whether paid or unpaid as a gift. The opportunity to raise children is also a gift. Work and parenthood are not mutually exclusive, but there will need to be give-and-take and an ebb and flow in different seasons of life. No one gets this completely right. May you find joy and peace, instead of anxiety, guilt, and struggle, as you work this out for yourself.

With very much love,
Amy

Becoming Lovers of Truth

Dear Jo,

In a recent conversation I had with an eminent scientist about the current state of the evangelical church, he described to me how the process of scientific peer review was underpinned by a healthy acknowledgment that fallible humans often delude themselves. We may so desperately want to come to a particular conclusion that our scientific research can become skewed and made to serve a particular end rather than follow the objective methods of scientific inquiry. Hence the need for peer review. Other voices and perspectives are needed to check our work and keep us honest. Accurate footnoting and transparent citation in academia and publishing play a similar role. Being subject to these levels of scrutiny is grueling and time-consuming but essential.

This friend speculated that these days a healthy appreciation of the fall of humanity, as described in Genesis 3, seems more at home in the scientific community than in many religious communities. Much of the evangelical church has lost hold of a healthy and biblical view of our capacity to sin, to self-deceive, and to promote our own interests above the pursuit of truth. This makes us susceptible to narcissistic leaders and bureaucratic cabals who take over churches, movements, communities, political parties, and organizations in the name of success, power, greater efficiency, or respectability while losing the very heart of the original mission and any connection with truth itself. No wonder so many people are walking away from organized religion and are disillusioned with large-scale operations.

Rather than giving in to this anti-intellectual bent, I want to suggest that Christians today are desperately in need of a reformed and reinvigorated Christian faith. A curious, honest, reflective faith that takes the time to read, learn, and discover. An intellectually honest and humble faith that welcomes questions and insights from tradition, culture, science, philosophy, and of course Scripture. This kind of faith can inspire and draw leaders and opinion formers to the person of Jesus. Many commitments and actions are needed for a generation to experience this kind of cultural and faith renewal. But certainly one of them is a commitment to truth whatever the cost.

Dorothy L. Sayers explores this idea in her popular novel *Gaudy Night*. Sayers was a close friend and contemporary of C. S. Lewis. She was among the first cohort of women to graduate from the University of Oxford in 1920. She became a leading female voice for Christianity in Britain in the first half of the twentieth century through her writing and broadcasting on the BBC.

(Spoilers ahead!)

Gaudy Night is set in Shrewsbury College, a fictional college for women not unlike the college Sayers attended. The novel explores the disruption of the community by a number of obscene disturbances that escalate toward an attempted murder. The plot turns on the fact that a young scholar, Miss De Vine, had written an essay exposing a small act of scholarly deception on the part of a male academic, who had suppressed a source that countered his thesis. The exposure had led to the termination of his academic career, with the devastating repercussions of his subsequent suicide being felt by his wife and children. His widow takes a job as a scout (a cleaner) at Shrewsbury College and is eventually unmasked as the perpetrator by the detective Lord Peter Wimsey.

Sayers later wrote, "By choosing a plot that should exhibit intellectual integrity as the one great permanent value in an emotionally unstable world I should be saying the thing that, in a confused way, I have been wanting to say all my life."[1]

When faced with the question in her own cultural context about the point of a university education, Sayers mused, "The integrity of mind that money cannot buy; the humility in face of the facts that self-esteem cannot corrupt: these are the fruits of scholarship, without which all statement is propaganda and all argument special pleading."[2]

Renewal within the church and wider society today will not be possible without this kind of honesty about truth. For Sayers, the highest possible value of truth, untarnished by self-interest, remained a real possibility in this imperfect world, but only Christian revelation could make it viable. She argued that the truth about God is accessible to those who pursue truth with integrity because God entered human history in Christ. She believed that Christ as embodied truth in history underpinned all other glimpses of truth in the wider world. I have learned so much from reading her work.

There is a crucial prerequisite for discovering truth: intellectual integrity. Those pursuing truth and those purporting to lead need to be reminded about the vested interests and personal costs that so often prevent us from actually following the evidence. As Christians, we need to look in the mirror before holding it up to the world and calling others to do the same.

I pray this generation of Christians recaptures a rigorous commitment to the integrity of truth as we navigate all kinds of power discourses within the church and wider culture. Truth matters. Humans are susceptible to self-deception, even in the cause of faith or something we consider to be the "greater good." The principles of intellectual integrity matter. Our very future as a faith community may hang on realizing this.

With hope,
Amy

LETTER 9

Embrace Curiosity

Dear Jo,

Today I returned to my favorite seat in the Radcliffe Camera, a library in Oxford where I fell in love with learning and where I first really experienced the light bulb moment of ideas falling into place. Seat 22 on the upper level of the library, by the window overlooking All Souls College, is a special place.

As a student studying theology, I had a lot of knowledge in distinct areas and was quite good at writing analytical essays. But the moment I first deeply grasped the essential interconnectedness and coherence of the Scriptures with history, philosophy, and reality happened here in this chair in 1997 when I was studying for my final exams. I had a eureka moment as knowledge and ideas I had held in discrete, separate columns came together and a big picture emerged for me.

This is a beautiful thing God does for those who seek him, and I think it can give us a profound sense of security *and* curiosity. In leadership, both security and curiosity come under fire, but both are needed if we are to become safe, interesting, or creative leaders and thinkers.

We can be safe and secure in something far greater than ourselves. There is a wider, bigger story, a narrative of God's relationship with humanity and this world, a story that makes sense of our own stories. I predict that as someone seeking out your place in the story you will find that this security will be tested. Don't be tempted to compare yourself to others. That pathway leads to insecurity and ultimately jealousy and discontentment. People who are uneasy in their own skin and story end up being dangerous to others. Resist the impetus to compare and compete. Find depth in God through prayer and study. Build those foundations deeply and consistently while you are young. I suggest a good hour or even two a day in study and prayer as a daily habit.

Curiosity may also come under fire. Christians can be narrow-minded and fearful, wary of doubt because of the path it may open to deconstruction.

But healthy curiosity means reading a wide range of literature, philosophy, early church writings, history, and textual commentaries. And Jesus promised that the Holy Spirit will lead us into all truth. So stay curious. Don't let any movement or denomination's subcultural blandness knock the life out of you.

If you ever feel a bit weird as a Christian woman drawn to depth and creativity, study and theology, literature and history, be encouraged that some have gone ahead of you and that those very characteristics and disciplines are vitally important and desperately needed for a life of dynamic leadership. They will serve you well as reservoirs to draw from and will prepare you for the long road.

Nurture your mind and imagination with the time you have now. You will find your soul and spirit fed too. In the long run, it will matter that you nurtured your theological depth and your creative curiosity.

With love from a few years ahead,
Amy

PART 3

Facing Chauvinism in Christian Spaces

On Being Female

Dear Jo,

Being a woman is glorious. The downsides are well-known, so I don't need to rehearse for you the challenges of menstrual pain, fertility worries, the fear and experience of assault, the pay gap, and many others. Today I write to you to celebrate who we are as women: our bodies, our capacities, our resilience, and our sisterhood.

Our bodies are amazing. Don't spend time and energy worrying about being thin or looking young. For one thing, in ten years' time you may very well look back on the shape and condition of your body and face now and rejoice in them. Why not enjoy them today as well? Your glorious body can do so much. You can bring forth life and grow it inside you. You can choose not to do that and for your brilliant menstrual cycle to carry away that preparation for life one month and restore it again the next. Your body has extraordinary capacity to bend and flex and run. Cultivate your body's health and ability to move, to get stronger, and to hold strength in its core. My athletic teenage son accompanied me to Pilates one day, having teased me about the level of exercise it provides. At the end of the session, he fainted. We're stronger and more resilient than we know. Nurture your body in ways that work for you.

Women have extraordinary capacity for the many dimensions of life, and we seem to be able to multitask across our spheres and to do many things at the same time. Not many men share this trait. Embrace your beautiful and complex world, from work strategy to looking after the people in your life. I predict that at the center of networks of flourishing people there will be capable women making life happen. Rather than resenting the demands on our time and attention or the weight of the emotional burden that falls to you, why not thrive on the way your capability for and generosity in living expansively connect you to people, causes, and places? Women make communities, businesses, churches, and families better places to be.

Women have awe-inspiring levels of resilience. This goes beyond our ability to give birth to children, often laboring for many hours in considerable pain. That same resilience is seen in the lives and careers of women in all kinds of settings. Overcoming disadvantage and prejudice, rising above physical limitations, and navigating societal conventions, women are building lives free from oppression. Women who have escaped situations of domestic violence or coercion show us strength.

Women can make life beautiful for themselves and others in the context of devastating loss. I recently met a woman who had come to Britain as a refugee from the war in Ukraine. Her husband is on the front line of the war, and she has not seen him for eighteen months other than on video calls. She has made a home for herself and her children and is working full-time to provide for them. She has learned English. I met her as she arrived at our farm, having taken a week of leave from her job to volunteer to cook the food for a holiday camp for 120 refugee children.

Women also have the ability to forge bonds of sisterhood and create networks of joy, support, and safety. Of course, men may have deep friendships and connections too. But it strikes me that women have an extraordinary capacity for this that makes the world a better place. Many male friendships are supported and maintained through the web and work of women's relationships. I have seen women gather around new mothers, celebrate career breakthroughs, support a grieving friend, prepare each other's children for university, and consistently plan social gatherings so that they and others can meet up. Women know how to show up for each other in the darkest days life can throw at us. We can be depended on, leaned on, cried with, and trusted with each other's pain. The friendships of women are beautiful and powerful.

It is glorious to be a woman, to meet other women and just know you share so many common experiences. I was recently in an airport and ahead of me was a woman traveling with two young children. She could not collapse her stroller and hold them both. She looked at me, and I offered her help. I said, "Whatever you need, I'm here. I've traveled with preschool twins." Her baby was willing to be held by me while she sorted everything out. I reassured her, "I'm not on your flight, but I know there will be women who will help you there too." I knew this was true because I had experienced it myself.

Let's rewrite the script in our minds. Yes, we need to fight oppression, and our safety is often at risk. But it is glorious to be a woman. The image of God is equally shared by male and female; without us, humanity is not complete. Celebrate the women in your life, and walk in the joy of knowing that it is a privilege to be a woman. There are so many blessings to be enjoyed.

With love,
Amy

When Others Are Threatened by You

Dear Jo,

I write to you today to acknowledge that simply being female will pose a threat to some of the people around you.

All my working life I have operated in spheres where women either were a minority or simply never had the opportunity to fulfill the kinds of roles I found myself in. I am grateful for the opportunities that my forebears couldn't have imagined. But I have also been reflecting on what it means to be an embodied woman in spaces where that is merely tolerated, ignored, or sometimes met with hostility. That I was the first woman to have certain opportunities led me to put up with things I would now question and resist. The constant balancing act—the effort to appease or at least not provoke powerful men—has additional layers when dealing with individuals who hold complementarian theologies and so operate on the basis that my work and calling are forbidden by God.

I understand that all hindsight is tinged with the cultural norms of today, but still, honest reflection is needed. I hope that hearing some of my story might help equip you for yours.

Early in my career, I was doing some work for a charity. The charity had invited me to serve specifically as a speaker. One day I was called to a meeting at the home of a leader in the charity. Once I sat down, he asked me how the work they had asked me to do could be squared with 1 Timothy 2. (Letter 13 will address this passage.) He was questioning whether my involvement as a woman was biblical. When others subsequently raised questions as to why less-qualified men were paid more by this same group to do similar work, the response was frosty. Why did I not quit collaborating with that group then and there? I do ask myself that now. But at the same time, I expected this to be the case. I could not fathom making a choice to walk away at that stage. In fact, it would have seemed self-indulgent to me.

Alongside experiences like this, wonderful godly men gave me opportunity after opportunity. I was the first woman to speak from the main platform of one of the most historic Bible conventions in the world. As I was climbing the stairs to the platform to preach, the dear individual who had made it possible for me to be there whispered, "You are the first woman to teach the Scriptures from this platform in over one hundred years. Don't mess it up!" The pressure was real.

We will all handle hostility differently. I have experienced male students skipping my lectures during courses I was teaching or turning up pointedly late without apology or explanation. I expected and accepted this resistance and rudeness and chose not to make a song and dance about them. My approach was to let the quality of my work speak for itself and resist being a "campaigner" for my rights.

But deep down, I knew I was not completely safe. I felt that reality for decades, and I don't want that for you. I don't want to contribute to a system that normalizes this expectation for women who teach and lead in both Christian and mainstream contexts, as both can be ripe for hostility toward women. More recently, the threats and trolls online have increased; this negativity doesn't seem to be getting better for your generation.

In my twenties and thirties, I suffered from a chronic illness: endometriosis. I continued to work through the pain, never taking a day off. Even when I needed surgery, I took the time as vacation. I felt that men in my workplace wouldn't understand this illness, as it's a female disease—not something I wanted to be common knowledge among my coworkers. The pain is indescribable, but I powered through. I lived and worked in an environment where I feared that sharing this pain would enable others to dismiss me as a weak woman.

This is not as it should be. Genesis 1:27 tells us that human beings were created in the image of God, "male and female." The female body matters, as it bears the image of God. I believed this in theory but didn't experience it in practice. There was a disconnect between my work, my intellectual life, my leadership, and my body. And when my body was in pain in a peculiarly female way, I did not feel there was grace for this, and so I bore it, hid it, and pushed through it.

How did the Christian faith, which blazed a trail in the ancient world for women to flourish, become a context where women's bodies are not celebrated or given their due respect? The early church fully released women and eventually turned how the Roman Empire viewed women on its head. In the empire, women were objects and possessions. Their voices and opinions didn't matter. Girl babies were often left to die because families wanted a boy; if they did not die, they were found and used as slaves—often sexual slaves. Instead of having the lowest status and being vulnerable to sexual slavery, women in the Christian world were educated and encouraged to serve. Women such as Phoebe, Lydia, and Junia played leading roles in the church. Women such as Perpetua and Felicity died for their faith as martyrs alongside men in the amphitheater, and their deaths were recorded as significant. Paul wrote that "there is neither Jew nor Greek, neither slave nor free, nor is there male and female, for you are all one in Christ Jesus" (Gal. 3:28). That vision changed the Roman world and left the West with a legacy of education and value for women.

It is time to recapture that vision and live it out in practice. May we minister, write, teach, and lead not in spite of our bodies but in and through the image-bearing life God has given us. And may we create communities that understand and empathize with female suffering without stigma or shame. Don't underestimate how different and freeing and powerful that would be for all of us as followers of Jesus.

It is time to challenge behaviors that belittle and undermine women in our churches and workplaces. I hope you will have the strength to stand up and resist unhealthy dynamics. I will join you.

With love,
Amy

Chauvinism

Dear Jo,

It isn't inspiring or encouraging to think about chauvinism, but I feel I need to write a letter to you about this distressing subject to help equip and prepare you. It may be that you will experience this directly or see it in the lives of those you love, support, and journey with. Over the course of my life and work, I have had to cope with it in various forms. From the stark threats and trolling to the more subtle but pervasive climate of nastiness toward women in many spheres, misogyny is alive and well in many leadership spaces. Unfortunately, preparing for leadership or any public-facing work means you need to be ready to face this kind of onslaught.

Some of the particular attacks that women face in Christian spaces are rooted in a deep antagonism toward women that finds cover in teaching and attitudes accommodated in some sections of the church. To withstand and stand up to these attitudes, we need to explore where the antagonism comes from and how it prospers.

The most significant misunderstanding leading to the degrading of women is the idea that the Bible positions Eve as a scapegoat. Much of Western art and literature sees the fall of Eve before Adam as the underlying basis for denigrating women. Regardless of whether this is a good interpretation of Scripture, the impetus to blame women for the wrongs of the world and to regard women with suspicion and disgust is pervasive across cultures. In a debate with an atheist scholar, I tried to make the argument that Genesis presents Eve as an autonomous person, an equal image bearer of God with Adam. The very fact that Eve exercises choice points to the equality and humanity of women. I am not sure how effective this argument was for her, but for me it is significant. When men view themselves as superior to women based on the creation narrative in Genesis, they are distorting the meaning of the text.

Another major area to consider is male and female roles. Mainstream complementarian teaching says that men and women are equal in status but different in role. This specifically applies to married women (and in some cases to daughters too) in the home. In the church, this applies to women regardless of marital status; women cannot lead or teach men and to varying degrees are limited to domestic or child-related roles of service. But the very idea of gender-based roles is culturally contextual and certainly not spelled out in Scripture. For example, my father is German and my mother is British. In Britain, males carve the meat for a meal. In Germany, carving is part of a traditionally female role. Who decides within the home what men and women can and cannot do? It is hard to see how many of these cultural preferences could be deemed as biblical.

The idea of a difference between male and female status and set roles in the home is rooted in 1 Corinthians 11:3: "But I want you to realize that the head of every man is Christ, and the head of the woman is man, and the head of Christ is God." There are many questions about what "headship" means. Is it hierarchical, and if so, does it then negate other Scripture passages about Christ being no less God than the Father? What about unmarried women? Are they subordinate to men? It seems more likely that Paul is using the word *head* in the way it originally occurred in Greek—to mean the source of a river. He is referencing the interdependence of men and women. In the Genesis account, Adam is the *source* of the creation of Eve, but Eve is Adam's *ezer*—often translated as "helper" (Gen. 2:18, 20). Elsewhere in Scripture, God is humanity's *ezer*, meaning "savior" or "deliverer" (e.g., Exod. 18:4; Deut. 33:7). *Ezer* is likely a reference to the prophecy that the Messiah will be born of a woman and not referring to a hierarchically inferior or domestic role.

Even if 1 Corinthians 11:3 does refer to some kind of leadership role in a marriage, it is hard to see why this would be extended to workplaces or ministry contexts; meanwhile, leadership in New Testament understanding always refers to service anyway. Jesus washed his disciples' feet and laid down his life for us as a demonstration of loving leadership. Also, going first (Adam being made before Eve) shouldn't be too important. After all, it was Jesus who said, "The first will be last" (Matt. 20:16).

If a biblical vision of the relationship between men and women does not allow for hierarchy, and the distinction of roles between men and women is culturally nuanced, what about church leadership? First Timothy 2 will be addressed in the next letter, but clearly the promise of Joel 2:28 that God will pour out his Spirit on men and women and that both will prophesy directly counters any denigration of women or minimizing of women in God's kingdom.

So where does the impetus to denigrate and dominate women come from? While many point to Genesis as the root of these ills, giving preferential status to men at the expense of women in all its forms is unbiblical. Genesis 1:27 speaks of male and female as equal image bearers of God. But God's judgment that comes as a result of the fall does help explain why chauvinistic attitudes persist. "He will rule over you" (Gen. 3:16) is a consequence of sin, a curse that describes reality in a fallen world, and not the aim of redemption. Jesus's death on the cross breaks the power and pattern of the curse. He redeems humanity. Male and female. The Christian life ought to reflect this freedom in Christ.

As a Christian, I believe there is no space for coercion, domination, or any act of violence against a woman. It is time not only to end the enslavement of women in the trafficking industry and the degradation of women in the sex industry but also to end violence against women in their homes. And it is time to release the full talents, skills, love, resources, empathy, creativity, and leadership of half of the population in the church. The church should be the first place that says no to chauvinism and that radically empowers women. In order to do that, we would need to recognize misogyny in all its guises and begin to actively resist it. The early church was known for this. May it be so again in our day.

While I want to warn you that attacks, spite, and hostility go with the territory of being a woman who leads, I also hope we can resolve to stand against such things with greater courage and urgency in our day. May our confidence in Christ spur us on.

With love,
Amy

How to Read 1 Timothy 2

Dear Jo,

I have been promising to write to you about 1 Timothy 2 in greater length, since it is such a significant passage for those who seek to limit women in professional and ministry roles. It is important for all who take the Scriptures seriously as the final authority for how we live and what we believe to grapple with texts in a genuine way.

Here's what the text says:

> A woman should learn in quietness and full submission. I do not permit a woman to teach or to assume authority over a man; she must be quiet. For Adam was formed first, then Eve. And Adam was not

the one deceived; it was the woman who was deceived and became a sinner. But women will be saved through childbearing—if they continue in faith, love and holiness with propriety. (1 Tim. 2:11–15)

Doesn't this text undermine the claims of egalitarians? And isn't the Bible clearly saying that women cannot teach or have authority over men?

I do not believe it does. A careful study of the words used and the context in which Paul wrote this letter helps us to see that Paul had not changed his mind from his joyous exclamation in Galatians 3:28, "There is neither Jew nor Greek, neither slave nor free, nor is there male and female, for you are all one in Christ Jesus."

From the broader letter to Timothy, we know that Paul is concerned that Timothy is ill with stomach complaints and other ailments (1 Tim. 5:23), and we can see that Paul is worried that Timothy wants to leave his posting in Ephesus, since Paul urges him to stay (1:3). It seems that heresy has broken out in the Ephesian church (4:1–3), so Paul needs to encourage Timothy to speak out against those who "forbid people to marry and order them to abstain from certain foods" (4:3).

Ephesus was the home of the Temple of Artemis, which is considered one of the seven wonders of the ancient world. Within the temple, women exercised power on two levels. The entire temple was controlled by a group of virgins and castrated men, and under their control were thousands of female priestess-slaves. Ephesus's entire socioeconomic structure was dominated by the goddess Artemis. Anyone living in Ephesus daily experienced the power of Artemis and her priestesses.

So goddess worship was controlled by virgins who shared leadership with males only if they were castrated. These individuals held authority over both men and women on the matters brought before them. Thus, it's helpful to ask, as New Testament scholar Kenneth Bailey does, "In such an atmosphere, what kind of female-male relations would have developed? What possibility would any male religious leadership have had for a sense of dignity and self-respect? What kind of female attitudes would have prevailed in such a city? How easy would it have been for the values of the society to have penetrated the church?"[1]

No church is going to be immune from the social, religious, economic, cultural, and political context of its location. The context of 1 Timothy, then, is a city in which religious female leaders of the local temple gained power through avoiding marriage and childbirth. It is interesting that precisely these themes are directly addressed by Paul in his letter to the Ephesian church. Timothy's congregation was not immune from the wider culture of the city or their specific experiences within it.

So let's examine the specific phrases of Paul's advice. "A woman should learn in quietness and full submission" (1 Tim. 2:11). Remember how radical Jesus was in encouraging Mary to sit at the feet of a rabbi and learn? The same restrictions on women in Judaism seem to have been common in Greco-Roman culture. Men sat at the feet of a teacher, and women focused on the domestic sphere (with the exception of Artemis's priestesses, who created a female sphere in the temple). Paul does not echo Martha's initial complaint and banish women to the kitchen; rather, he lets women learn . . . in quietness and submission. Paul's emphasis in the letter on "sound doctrine" as opposed to heresy gives us the answer as to what they are to submit to. Women need to learn good, solid theology in an atmosphere of tranquility.

"I do not permit a woman to teach or to assume authority over a man; she must be quiet" (1 Tim. 2:12). Priscilla taught Apollos (Acts 18:26), every reader of Luke 1:46–55 has been instructed by Mary, and everyone who has heard and believed the words of Jesus in John 14:24–27 has been taught by Martha. If we believe in the crucifixion and resurrection narratives in the Gospels, we have been taught by women. The women prophets of Corinth (1 Cor. 11:5) and Caesarea (Acts 21:9) spoke and built up the church with their encouraging prophecies. And so Paul is writing, "I do not permit *these* (heretical) women (in Ephesus) to teach," and then he goes on, "or to assume authority over a man."

The key Greek word translated here as "authority" is *authenteō*, which means more accurately "to lord it over." It appears only here in the New Testament. Elsewhere in Greek literature, it is a very strong word and could also be translated as "to commit murder," "to assert absolute sway," or "to usurp authority." The Syriac Peshitta New Testament (fourth century) translates this word with *mamraha*. The root of this word has to do with insolence and bullying.[2] These heretical women are to stop making misleading claims within the newly formed Ephesian church.

Paul continues: "For Adam was formed first, then Eve. And Adam was not the one deceived; it was the woman who was deceived and became a sinner" (1 Tim. 2:13–14). There seems to be a direct contradiction here with Galatians 3:28, where Paul says that in Christ there is no male and female.

Early church father John Chrysostom is helpful here in suggesting how to understand this invocation of the creation order of the man and the woman. Chrysostom draws a connection between Romans 5 and this text. "After the example of Adam's transgression . . . so here the female sex transgressed, not the male. As all men died through one (Adam) because that one sinned, so the whole female race transgressed because the woman was in the transgression."[3]

Perhaps the Artemis-influenced female heretics in the church in Ephesus had very little knowledge of the Jewish Scriptures and did not know the role Eve played in the fall of humanity. As new Christians from an Artemis-worshiping background, they had heard Paul's first Adam / second Adam teaching in which original sin is explained as being in Adam and redemption is explained as being in Christ. These women who need to learn some theology had perhaps repeated this, without referencing Eve's role in the fall, as a way to demean men in the church. And so here Paul is encouraging Timothy to correct them. "The woman was deceived and became a sinner" was an important theological nuance to introduce. Chrysostom helps us to see how the early church fathers understood this text.

And then this section concludes with the sentence "But women will be saved through childbearing—if they continue in faith, love and holiness with propriety" (1 Tim. 2:15). The word "saved" here is the Greek *sōzō*. Paul seems to be saying that alongside his cherished justification by faith there is now another route to salvation for women, and that is through bearing children. This text could mean that there will be one moment of childbirth that will save us all—Mary giving birth to Jesus. Or this sentence could be addressing the female heretics who were teaching other women not to bear children. If this is the case, then the verb *sōzō* (save) could also be translated "to have good health." Childbearing is not an unspiritual or defiling act, as the women in Artemis's temple taught. Childbirth is a blessing and brings blessing. Women who bear children are not diminished or demeaned.

Understanding the challenges of the Ephesian context helps us to interpret this passage in line with the rest of Paul's own teaching in the New Testament as well as Jesus's example.

I am indebted to Ken Bailey for his research and writing on this subject. His engagement with the evidence, including Middle Eastern languages and ancient culture, opened my eyes to how this text should best be read. I hope you can see that 1 Timothy 2 is not a blanket disqualification for women to work, minister, lead, and teach in equality with men.

With every blessing,
Amy

PART 4

Pursuing Leadership Success

Learn to Say Yes!

Dear Jo,

Have you ever noticed that when opportunities for you to lead arise, something inside you holds you back? Perhaps you feel reluctant to go for a promotion at work or hesitant to say yes to a new opportunity.

Christine Exley of Harvard Business School and her colleague Judd Kessler found in their research that women are far less likely to self-promote than men and that women rate their own potential more harshly than men do. For example, when both a man and a woman know they answered fifteen out of twenty questions correctly, the woman is more likely to describe her performance less favorably than the man.[1] After all the progress that has been made in some cultures, women are still less likely to take advantage of opportunities. I believe this will be even more true for those raised or working in a church or ministry setting.

I am writing to you today to encourage you to say yes more often to the opportunities that come to you. I know in my own working life that I have agonized over saying yes to opportunities to travel, or speak on large platforms, or take on board positions when offered them. Sometimes I have counted myself out for seemingly practical reasons. "I can't be away from home because of the needs of my family." At other times, the reluctance has been "I'm not sure I have enough experience to fulfill the role." One of the biggest blessings of my life has been a husband who champions me and has believed in my work more than I ever have. He has been the one to say, "They asked you, and so they must think you have the experience for the board role" or "I will step up at home and with the children for those few days so you can travel. You should go." I want to encourage you today to say yes to opportunities when they come instead of immediately thinking of all the reasons to say no.

Saying yes to opportunities will mean preparing yourself on several levels. First, saying yes may require you to step outside your comfort zone. It is rarely comfortable to take on new responsibilities in work or ministry. Saying yes might mean extending yourself beyond what you have achieved before, being tested in new ways, working hard, facing new physical challenges, and dealing with nerves. Staying within the zone of what we know we can manage often feels easier. But stepping out of my comfort zone has always ended up with God meeting me in my weakness and expanding my terrain in some way. Without the prayer, preparation, worry, and work, I don't think I would have grown in the way I have. I think of the first ministry trip I took to Australia. I was really worried about being so far from home, especially for ten days away from my family. But that trip ended up creating all kinds of opportunities and connections, and it enabled me to visit the land of my birth for the first time and to visit family members and others who knew my parents when I was born.

Second, saying yes to opportunities may mean that you begin to operate in a wider geographical sphere than before. That will likely involve travel. This is a genuine consideration, since travel takes a toll on the body and consumes significant time, whether in a regular commute or in one-off trips. For me, travel has often been difficult because I suffer from motion sickness and a back issue. But travel has also been a source of blessing, as I have encountered outstanding leaders, seen beautiful places, and fulfilled dreams of visiting various wonders of the world. I encourage you to take the opportunities, including those that involve travel. Even a commute can be a time to reflect, decompress, make calls, or listen to a podcast or read a book that restores you.

Third, saying yes to opportunities might also involve making practical arrangements at home. The unseen labor of making your home life work when new opportunities come needs to be factored in, but don't let this hold you back. You can do it! I know that saying yes to opportunities means the laundry will be up to the ceiling and the fridge I had lovingly stocked will be empty when I return from a trip. But I have learned that the practical needs I am responsible for can be taken care of if I plan things well and in advance.

Finally, saying yes to opportunities might mean that you need extra grace and strength to handle the opinions of others. Jealousy might prompt some to assume you are getting above your station, or others might fear you are leaving them behind. The judgments that women who achieve great things face are real, but they don't really matter in the end. The truth is you are not pushy or proud or unfeminine for stepping into opportunities that are open to you.

I'm cheering you on and hoping you will find the courage more often to say yes.

With very much love,
Amy

Who Gets the Credit?

Dear Jo,

In an effort to put the good of a cause ahead of your need for acknowledgment, have you ever found yourself saying, "It doesn't matter who gets the credit"? If you have, you are like many women I know.

After many years in international ministry and leadership, I have noticed that gifted women in organizations, workplaces, and churches, motivated by a godly desire to serve and to be humble like Jesus, tend to adopt a posture of humility and to deflect praise and even basic recognition. But I have also seen that this impetus can have disastrous consequences.

Women may find that their ideas and work are easily commandeered by men—some of whom genuinely seem to believe that the work they are taking credit for should be attributed to them. Women who have worked in diverse settings, from banks to universities to the White House, have noticed this phenomenon.

It was widely reported that during the first Obama administration, senior women officials noticed that their ideas were often adopted and commandeered by male colleagues. Some of these women devised a strategy called "amplification," which entailed hammering across one another's points during meetings. After a woman offered an idea, if it wasn't acknowledged, another woman would repeat it and give her colleague credit for suggesting it. "I agree with the analysis Rachel just offered. Should we work some more on Rachel's idea?"[1] The president noticed and took steps to make sure women were listened to and credited for their con-tributions. As a result of this, women in Washington and then in communities and workplaces across the country decided to adopt the strategy as their own, and amplification has become a positive way women can support one another in the workplace.

Within church settings, women often hold back, fearful of com-ing across as too brash or pushy if they take credit for their work. Many of us have been taught that to be demure is the same as biblical humility. Yet Jesus commended women who stepped up and exercised faith. Their contribution to the church is recorded in the Gospels. Biblical humility puts the good of the cause and the good of the team above our own preferences and comfort, but it does not erase us.

In truth, teams produce the best outcomes when people honor each other. Taking the credit for another person's work does not serve the team or the cause. If this kind of behavior goes un-checked, decisions and budgets will be made by people who mis-understand who actually does most of the work, who is gifted to come up with key ideas that deliver for the organization, or who can pull thriving, happy teams together. Long term, credit tak-ers throw everything out of balance, and everyone suffers. Those whose service or gifts go unrecognized find themselves unable to move forward, as the wind is taken out of their sails. False credit taking also damages the credit taker in the end; although they may benefit in the short term, they are not able to offer what others are now trusting them to deliver. Deception may cover this for a while, but eventually the truth catches up, and people at every level in the organization begin to realize the person lacks substance. Sadly, frustration can then boil over into resentment and dissatisfaction.

So when you feel tempted to let credit takers steal the recognition you are due, pause for a moment. It won't be biblical humility that lets this slide. Perhaps it would be better if you, with all humility, clearly and honestly state your perception of who did what, amplify the contributions of everyone on the team, and remember that you too are made in the image of God and so your work and your name matter.

With very much love,
Amy

Watch Out for the Narcissist

Dear Jo,

I woke up in the middle of the night with a strong sense that I should write to you with a warning. As you continue to grow in confidence and people see your competence and giftedness, you need to protect yourself from the narcissistic leader who may want to harness or marshal your strengths, resources, abilities, and energy for their own ends.

Watch out for the leader who says things like "Come and work with me and write your own job description," offers you overly generous compensation, or engages in flattery. These may indicate a narcissist who love bombs at first in an effort to reel you in. If something seems too good to be true, it probably is. Look out for the leader who operates with a mindset of exceptionalism: "We are the only ones who understand this" or "Very few people are like us and able to operate at this level." This sounds appealing at first, but the narcissist believes that only they are exceptional. Flattery can be a ploy to draw you in to working for their agenda and end, with no actual concern for your development or gifts.

I have learned the hard way that while the diligent and conscientious are susceptible to anxiety, we can also become easy prey for the leader who has an impressive veneer. This is the entertaining, affable narcissist who can talk their way into one-off displays of effectiveness. But dig a bit deeper, and they have a limited perspective, an inflated backstory, and just enough charisma to distract from their lack of substance, qualifications, or experience.

When the narcissist senses that people are realizing the emperor has no clothes, watch out for these red flags:

> *Aggression*: The switch from charm to anger is fierce. You are the problem if you question things, and you need to be silenced and smeared so that others will not listen to you. This may well come as a shock because it flies in the face of the affable persona they have built up. But regular, frightening flashes of anger are a warning sign that all is not well.
>
> *Distraction*: They may attempt to stop you from focusing on the specifics of what is concerning you and try to get you to look instead at some smaller, unrelated issue. Narcissists use this tactic to throw anyone off the scent of the major issues they are responsible for. Look out for leaders who present themselves as the rescuer of every situation,

swooping in to sort things out, when a closer look shows they are responsible for causing much of the chaos in the first place. They distract attention from a situation to buy enough time to enter as the savior figure.

Disinformation: Confusing and disconcerting mischaracterizations pulled off with supreme confidence in the moment may turn out to be false. Narcissistic leaders may be verbally gifted, dominating any room they are in with their observations and insights. The sheer volume of statements can make it difficult to discern a pattern of disinformation. Taking careful notes of meetings will help you recognize what is happening.

If possible, disentangle yourself from such a person at the earliest opportunity. Consider carefully if you are in a position and have the right support and resources to challenge them. Make sure you have solid records and factual evidence. When you challenge, do it kindly and patiently and in the presence of witnesses.

In all likelihood, the narcissist will ignore what you say and try to focus your attention on other things to evade the challenge you are bringing.

First, they may make the case that they are not offended that you raised an issue—they just take issue with the *way* you did it. They will attempt to move the focus from the issue at hand to *how* you brought the challenge. Your character and motives may be called into question. They may quote Matthew 18 in an effort to make the issue a two-sided interpersonal conflict with wrong on each side.

A second response is appeals to pity. They may focus on issues of outside perception and image management. They might say something like "This will make me and the organization look bad, and that will have terrible consequences for me / my family / the ministry." This is especially effective if the individual is widely appreciated.

A third response is threats and intimidation. "If you persist with your challenge, you will experience negative consequences." The threat might be specific or subtle, but the impact is devastating. Financial, legal, and relational costs are frightening and may be used to dissuade you from speaking up.

A fourth response is harassment. This is when things like mediation or reconciliation are weaponized. They may force you to sign a legal agreement that silences you if you receive severance, verbally bully you, or contact your friends and network in order to disparage your professional and personal reputation if you persist with your viewpoint rather than acquiescing to theirs.

By contrast, a biblical response to an honest and evidence-based challenge begins with openness. A leader should have a posture that if they sinned or hurt others, they want to know so they can put things right and repent. If there is misunderstanding and they have not done anything wrong, they are still sorry they made you feel as you do and acknowledge your hurt. They offer evidence as to why things aren't quite as you thought.

Another aspect of a biblical response to challenge is humility. The leader acknowledges their own propensity to sin, their fallibility, and their blind spots and weaknesses, and they welcome the opportunity to repent, learn, and clear up misunderstanding. They may not agree with the challenge, but they are willing to listen to hard things and weigh the substance of the challenge. Their personhood is not challenged, and their responses are kind, even when they disagree with someone.

Another characteristic is love. The leader does not subject you to negative consequences if you say what you think. They continue to extend love and mercy to you.

As you grow as a leader, guard your own heart against narcissism. Flee from toxic setups that will harm you even though they may promise platform and opportunity. Offer love and kindness to people, including those you find difficult.

As I think of you today, I want you to know that learning these lessons for yourself may be painful. But you will be okay. The Lord will carry you through, and hopefully this letter will serve as a reminder that you are not alone.

With all my love,
Amy

LETTER 17

Shortcuts and Storms

Dear Jo,

I'm sitting by Padstow Harbor in Cornwall, England, the morning after a storm whipped through the country. We were battered with high winds and surging sea, but today all is calm. The water is still, as if nothing happened. The fishing boats are safely moored. This village has been inhabited for generations. Seasons and storms have come and gone. I think of you and me and am reminded of the words of Jesus to his disciples about building on a rock rather than on sand.

A building without a foundation is quickly put up and may look impressive; the growth is fast and the builder might be regarded as efficient, productive, and proficient—that is, until a storm comes along and everything collapses. Building on a rock base takes much longer, and the unseen strength of the foundation is revealed only when the storm whips through.

Both builders experience a storm. In Jesus's expectations for us as disciples, storms are certainties. Experiences and circumstances that batter, shake, overwhelm, or flood us are not a sign that God has abandoned us. Storms will come.

The question to ask yourself is whether what you are building in life has the foundation to stay standing. The unglamorous work of foundation building—time spent studying the Word, praying, fasting, serving, and working in thankless and unspectacular king-dom endeavors—will matter. Time given to discipling, encouraging, praying for, equipping, cooking for, and eating with those we lead and serve is not wasted. Don't rush on to what seems more important.

Jesus uses another image for our lives. He says that fire will come and test our work and that what is hay, straw, or wood will burn—but what remains is gold.

A great storm came upon the teams I collaborated with in a global organization a number of years ago (more on that experi-ence in the next section of letters). The same happened in many highly visible megachurches in recent years. Impressive-looking things are being swept away in floods and burned up in fires. Management systems, fundraising techniques, buildings, power hierarchies, organizational charts, and the reputations of some who were greatly admired—all this was destroyed. These things are burned up when deception, love of money, the use of fear to coerce and dominate, and cowardice are uncovered.

Yet the foundations formed by faithful servants will remain. Evangelism, service, people pastored in small groups, friendships formed, prayers prayed, thoroughly researched apologetics published, young people equipped and inspired in the faith, leaders of character and integrity: this carries forward. Impressive organizations, with their hierarchies, money, celebrities, and platforms, are collapsing. But anything that is good, beautiful, and true in the lives and nations of those who built for the Lord remains—refined by fire, humbled and less resourced, but still standing.

As you lead and live for Christ today, may I encourage you? If you are in a storm or a fire, know that the New Testament tells us to expect these things (Matt. 7:24–27; 1 Cor. 3:15). Throw yourself on the Lord and trust him.

If you are not yet in a storm, build in a way that anticipates what will come. Don't cut any ethical corners. Conduct yourself with integrity—financially, ethically, morally—in your speech and actions. Build intentionally on the Bible, with habits of prayer and service. Don't be distracted by the glamorous, the quick, or the ministries or churches that appear from nowhere and seem to have money that endlessly flows.

It is worth putting the unseen, uncelebrated work of foundation building in now—you will be so thankful you did when the storm or fire comes.

I'm cheering you on and praying for your life to be marked by kingdom work that honors Christ—and lasts.

With very much love,

Amy

PART 5

Addressing Abuse and Injustice

My Experience in an Abuse Crisis

Dear Jo,

In the next few letters, I am going to be writing about some of the painful leadership lessons I learned through an abuse scandal involving a beloved Christian leader. The letters to come will also draw on what I learned through trying to support others in similar situations. Sharing this is not easy. I have made many mistakes and picked up some deep wounds along the way. I share my insights with you in the hope that they might be useful. For today, here is a brief outline of my experience.

I worked in the United Kingdom for Ravi Zacharias International Ministries (RZIM), which was part of the ministry of apologist Ravi Zacharias. I had many roles over a long period of time. I was the program director and then codirector of a center for Christian apologetics that received funds to provide scholarships for people from all over the world to study at Wycliffe Hall, Oxford, where I was also an associate tutor. It was an amazing privilege to serve under Dr. Michael Green and Professor Alister McGrath and alongside Dr. Os Guinness and Dr. John Lennox.

I learned so much from them and the many other scholars who visited and supported the work.

For several years, I also led a team of evangelists from across Europe, the Middle East, and Africa whose country directors received funding and support from Zacharias's ministry. These were outstanding individuals, serving God in their nations. Our focus was on the work we were doing, and as I was based in the United Kingdom and traveling and speaking I did not have much direct contact with Zacharias. I saw him at team gatherings and fundraising events, but due to his ostensible adherence to the Billy Graham rule (the idea that male Christian leaders are never to be alone with a woman other than an immediate family member), we did not interact on a personal level alone or communicate by email one-on-one. Zacharias was always kind, generous, and courteous in the interactions we had. He was an inspirational but distant figure.

When allegations arose that Zacharias had misrepresented his academic credentials and connection to various academic institutions, I was gravely concerned. Along with numerous team members, I asked for him and RZIM to apologize and set the record straight. I was able to apologize to our local partners on behalf of the United Kingdom organization. The cultural differences between the US and Europe were cited as factors, as was Zacharias's heritage, to explain how his credentials had been exaggerated. A first experience of difficulty for me was that my loyalty and charitable spirit were called into question in a few meetings where this issue was discussed. But in the busyness of work and life, I failed to interrogate this further and accepted Zacharias's statements of regret at face value.

When allegations of an online abusive sexual relationship were made against Zacharias, just over a year later, I was troubled by his narrative—that the accuser was an extortionist seeking $5 million—and the repeated reassurances from my seniors that the matter had been fully investigated by the board and Zacharias's denomination. We were consistently informed that both bodies had found him innocent of wrongdoing.

The questions and concerns that I and others raised during this period became the basis for a distrust in us, which was later to escalate into accusations of disloyalty and gossip. This happened despite the fact that I, to my great regret, eventually accepted the reassurances that the matter had been fully investigated by the two bodies to whom Zacharias was accountable and that he had been exonerated. The reassurances turned out to be completely untrue.

After Zacharias's death in 2020, moves began to be made to remove me from the organization. I was summoned to a conciliation meeting with an outside party to discuss "conflict" within the organization. The conciliation was largely focused on me as the problem person, and a major issue was that I had not trusted Zacharias regarding the allegations and had encouraged others to ask questions. I was threatened and subjected to psychological abuse over the course of four days. Within weeks, *Christianity Today* published an in-depth investigative piece exposing Zacharias's abuse of multiple women in several spa settings.[1]

A number of colleagues advocated for a genuinely independent investigation into Zacharias and the allegations of sexual abuse and the honest publication of those investigations. This was enormously challenging and required the exertion of pressure. People were fired and others were threatened. Following a false start with a law firm connected to Zacharias's personal representation, eventually a genuinely independent law firm was appointed. The report found that Zacharias had sexually abused women in spas as well as in other settings, and, following additional pressure from courageous individuals within the organization, the unredacted findings were published.[2]

As this was unfolding, I and others were able to speak with victims and apologize for not doing more to uncover the truth sooner. We also undertook a process of learning and repentance. Leading activists and thinkers in the areas of abuse and organizational cover-up gave us their time and expertise. The United Kingdom board of the organization separated from the RZIM global organization due to its inadequate response to systemic failings.

Receiving the forgiveness and love of Zacharias's victim who had been painted by the organization as an extortionist seeking a payout has been one of the biggest blessings of my life. Expressing public support for and belief in her a couple weeks later was an important step for me. I also agreed to the termination of my role and have since continued to seek and advocate for repentance and learning about organizational dynamics around abuse. I have been able to help and support victims of sexual and spiritual abuse in other organizational contexts as well in a range of cases.

I have been attacked by some for not doing enough soon enough, and I agree that this is where my failures lie. Learning about blindness to abuse in those who are connected to abusers has helped me understand how difficult it is to see the possibility of a beloved religious figure being a fraud. I have also been criticized for speaking up and being a part of the group of people who used our voices and resources to shine light into the darkness. I understand the pain driving this critique, since many wonderful people and ministries were impacted by the collapse of the organization. I have had to come to terms with both critiques.

As my eyes began to open to what was happening, I felt I had to raise questions and use my voice to push for transparency and accountability. Those who walked this path in different ways are some of the most heroic people I have ever met. I have not always gotten things right, but I hope that what I have learned may be of some use in your journey.

I pray you never need to address abuses of power in your own professional setting, but I fear you might. If you do, remember Jesus's promise that he came to fulfill Isaiah's prophecy of a Messiah who would loosen the chains of injustice and bind up the brokenhearted. This is Jesus's way.

With love,
Amy

When Institutions Cover Up Abuse

Dear Jo,

This is a letter I never wanted to write. When I think of you and your generation, I want you to be filled with hope and optimism about where God is calling you to lead. But it is important for me to share some thoughts on abuse in the church with you because you likely will need to stand up against evil and help rebuild safer, healthier structures for Christian communities.

A while ago I was having coffee with a dear friend in her home. We were catching up on life when she suddenly said, "I need to tell you something." Decades earlier as a young woman, she had been abused by a ministry leader. She had spoken up at the time but had been ignored and eventually was asked to leave. She had restarted her life in a different city because everyone had supported the leader. We wept together and then talked through her options: How to make a historic report. Who the legal authorities over this man were and how to approach them. What counseling she might want and what support I could offer. The most significant thing for her in that moment was to be believed.

I find myself asking what it is about people like me—people who have faith—that leaves us susceptible to such abuse and cover-up. How did it come to be that Christian faith, which exploded in the first and second centuries among the poor and marginalized, has produced institutions that have become breeding grounds for sexual abuse? It is sickening to realize that what ought to be the safest places, communities of faith where all human beings are prized as divine image bearers with sacred dignity and loved by God, are at times profoundly unsafe.

Jennifer Freyd, a psychologist and the founder of the Center for Institutional Courage, writes about "betrayal blindness" and institutional betrayal. She notes that having already experienced the abuse, a sufferer may then also be faced with a toxic institutional response.[1]

First, she points out that institutions with clear ideals of membership or belonging allow for the "othering" of anyone who makes an allegation so that the nonconforming attributes of such an individual can be highlighted in order to cast doubt on the veracity or importance of their testimony. Time and time again I have seen this happen in faith contexts. The person speaking up or the whistleblower is cast as an outsider who cannot be trusted and is smeared as a gossip. Something in their sexual, relational, or theological history makes them dubious. One organization that had promised to investigate allegations of abuse also hired people to run background checks to find dirt on the individuals coming forward.

Another common reaction is for institutions to point to their own prestige to assuage doubts raised by accusations made. This may involve displays of theological learning, a historic track record, significant attendance, or an emphasis on connections to trusted influencers in the field.

Another dysfunctional response is persistent blindness that is expressed as a "not knowing." Members of an organization conveniently maintain an unawareness of injustices, particularly if knowledge would be threatening to an office holder or the institution's well-being. This "intentional ignorance" looks very much like the foundation of a future legal defense based on a lack of knowledge, when it is an obvious duty of any leader in a context where allegations are being made to be as informed as possible.

In another case I know of, leaders insisted that all staff working for the Christian organization not read news reports, investigative pieces, leaked documents, or the testimony of victims. When staff members tried to point out that the evidence for the resurrection of Jesus was based on eyewitness accounts and that Christian faith is about public truth, they were chastised and told not to read or share anything that leaders hadn't vetted. This cult like behavior couched in the language of respect for authority was a huge red flag.

Finally, Freyd warns that we watch out for DARVO. This refers to a reaction that perpetrators of wrongdoing, particularly sexual offenders, may display in response to being held accountable for their behavior. The perpetrator may Deny the behavior, Attack the individual doing the confronting, and Reverse the roles of Victim and Offender such that the perpetrator assumes the victim role and turns the true victim—or the whistleblower—into an alleged offender.[2]

Knowing how to recognize these signs and call them out is the beginning of resisting toxic and damaging institutional patterns. This takes great courage, but it is the road to freedom.

Is there any hope for people of faith who care about the abuse of God's children when the church in its institutional form has failed miserably? I find hope in the words of Jesus Christ: "If anyone causes one of these little ones . . . to stumble, it would be better for them to have a large millstone hung around their neck and to be drowned in the depths of the sea" (Matt. 18:6).

The suffering of "little ones" matters to God at a profound level. According to Christ, ultimate accountability is coming. It is unavoidable, and it's an outworking of love. The promised judgment of evil underscores the value of the victim and offers a profound assurance for all who suffer: a loving God will hold the wicked to account, even when human institutions fail.

But this framework of judgment and justice also ought to be reflected in our commitments to each other today within faith communities. Transparency and accountability should be welcomed. The oversight of authorities is needed with regard to abuse and safeguarding. These things reflect an honest appraisal of the possibility of evil within our own camps and the necessity of proper evaluation. They demonstrate a healthy theological appreciation of our own human capacity to sin, to self-deceive, and to promote our own interests above the pursuit of truth. They demonstrate that we believe in the fall described in Genesis 3 and that we do not regard ourselves or our communities as being outside the scope of that chapter of the Bible. When considering whether to work in an organization, it is worth questioning whether this kind of oversight is in place.

As we look at what is happening in the church right now, with leaders' abuse being uncovered, it seems a reckoning is coming and that it's time for some tables to be overturned in our churches and institutions. The pursuit of power, the protection of assets, and the insinuations of lawyers and insurers that there is a "greater good" than bringing the truth into the light must be called out. Those who experienced danger in a place where they rightly expected to find safety are raising their voices. May they find in Christ one who prizes the "little ones." And may we be people who are willing to pay a personal cost to speak up for them.

With love,
Amy

When a Leader We Respect Harms Others

Dear Jo,

On hearing of the abuse perpetuated by a much-loved leader, I find myself reflecting on the unwanted lessons of the last few years. As I write to you today, I want to begin by acknowledging the disorientation and horror that rightly form the basis of a healthy reaction to hearing that a leader we respect, especially a Christian one, has abused others.

In this kind of situation, we might feel a theological impulse to rush to hope, seeking some kind of redemptive purpose or outcome to the situation. I vividly remember the words of a Christian lawyer who has represented many victims of sexual abuse and who spoke directly to me about this. I had found myself disoriented by the disappointing and woeful response of a trusted leader to allegations of sexual abuse. I kept hoping that if they were presented with specific information or arguments that they would surely respond differently. The lawyer stopped me midsentence and said, "Amy, I'm going to say something hard for you to hear. As an evangelical, you are wired for the redemption story. You believe in repentance, transformation, and new birth, and so you see that possibility everywhere, including where you shouldn't."

He went on to explain how abusive structures are propped up by Christians. He taught me that because believers are so shaped by the gospel and its potential, we believe redemption is possible in every situation. But that is not always healthy. In fact, oftentimes that very belief can be weaponized against us and our communities in order to cover up abuse. He mentioned that in all the cases of clergy sexual abuse that he had worked on in his practice, he had experienced Christian leaders coming to court to give evidence only in support of the character of the perpetrator and never on behalf of the victims. He showed me that I needed to sit in the disorientation and horror. I needed to dwell in lament and face the reality of the darkness. I needed to stop rushing on to the hope of a better outcome in order to truly confront the injustice and wrongdoing. I needed to face reality.

An unhealthy response when the abuse of an admired leader is uncovered is the rush to platitudes. "There but for the grace of God go I." My response to this now is "Are you saying you are in danger of raping women or assaulting children? No! We must do better. Please do not minimize the harm done to precious people who bear the image of God." Abuse is different from "falling into sin" or the other cozy metaphors that have arisen around sexual misconduct. The systemic, calculated nature of predation changes the level of disorientation we experience whether we fall prey to it directly or we suffer in the wider fallout in a community of faith. It is hard to fathom that someone we admired for their faith or leadership or skill in ministry or we found likeable and fun to be around set out systematically to groom and harm another person. I have learned that an important starting place in response is to accept the plausibility of what is alleged, with an expectation that evidence and due process will uncover the truth, and to acknowledge and lament the extent of the harm and damage done.

Another tendency related to misplaced hope among Christians is to focus on grace for the perpetrator of harm. "We are all sinners. Let's have grace for (the abuser)." Offering support or empathy to the leader we know rather than the person or people who have been harmed is surprisingly common. When this happens, the redemption story of the Bible is robbed of its true power, since repentance is skipped over and the powerful are upheld in their wrongdoing in the name of grace. The victims are often nameless and faceless to the community, whereas the accused is a beloved leader who has provided personal benefit or blessing to us. Can I ask that when you hear of a crisis of abuse that you pray for and empathize with those coming forward after having been harmed?

Jesus as the Good Shepherd left the ninety-nine sheep to search for the one who was lost. The one who is small, lost, insignificant, or out of sight is of inordinate value to our God. Any opportunity to be like him is worth taking. May we continue to grow into being his disciples.

By resisting the impetus to rush to hope and redemption, we follow a biblical pattern of acknowledging reality. When I was in a time of deep questioning and at my lowest point regarding the organization I had worked for, a more mature Christian came alongside me and took me to the beginning of Acts. He pointed out that the book does not go smoothly from the ascension of Jesus in chapter 1 to Pentecost in chapter 2. There is an entire section in between that I had often skipped over dedicated to the question of how to respond to the defection and betrayal of Judas. The casting of lots in order to replace one of the twelve is recounted. Luke does not find it necessary to edit out the devastating failure of one of the twelve disciples and the distress that his subsequent suicide must have caused his closest friends. The Bible contains a detailed account of how the church worked through Judas's absence and chose a new person to take on his role.

As Christians, we are not required to rush forward to Pentecost, to victory, without processing the pain of devasting failures and harms done to us and our community. These darker periods should not and need not be written out of our faith story. We need to spend time in truth telling and lament.

With love,
Amy

"What about All the Good the Leader Did?"

Dear Jo,

On hearing of the abuse perpetrated by a much-loved leader, we might find ourselves asking, "Where is God in this?" Or more precisely "How can I process my own good and even my spiritually significant experiences if the person God seemed to use in my life turns out to be an abuser?" Why would God let someone who is destroying people's lives be the source of blessing and encouragement for others?

I'll be honest—these are deeply troubling questions. I certainly don't have all the answers, but I hope some of these reflections might be helpful.

Let me begin by saying that I don't think the answer "We are all sinners" or "God uses broken people" cuts it when we are talking about patterns of abuse. While of course it is true that God blesses and uses imperfect people, in the case of abuse this can feel like a minimizing of the pain experienced by all who have been directly harmed. It falsely equates a mistake or missing the mark with intentional predation and harm. It also implies that abuse isn't of the greatest importance to God. This cannot be right.

So where might we begin?

Perhaps the perpetrator was on a journey and when the Lord worked through them in a way that blessed you or others, they had not yet taken the turn toward darkness, misuse of power, or abuse. And so, the blessing of God through their ministry was limited to the time before they intentionally embarked on the path of harm. It could also be the case that as they were starting on the road of wrongdoing, God continued to call them to repentance and gave grace for a limited period. Abuse coming to light is that window closing.

A second factor to consider is how much of what was meaningful to you was from God or others in a team, church, or conference rather than the individual. A theology of common grace means that the truth is the truth whoever declares it. Even the heavens declare the glory of God according to the psalmist. The grace of the life of the Spirit that you experienced far exceeds the involvement of an individual. What was good, beautiful, and true was from God, not the man or woman you received it from. Examples of this in apologetics, evangelism, church leadership, or preaching can be seen in the fact that very little of what one individual writes or says is completely original. The origin is the truth or reality itself. We humans are just proclaimers; the truth and life of the Spirit are bigger than any human mouth that shares them.

A third thing to wrestle with is the uncomfortable truth that the New Testament warns us that wolves will come among God's people (Acts 20:28–31; 2 Tim. 3:2–7). The wolves will get inside communities of faith and wreak havoc and destruction. This might feel like a discouraging point. You may find yourself wondering whether you can trust any religious context ever again. But you may find a strange comfort in the fact that Scripture warns us that people, presenting as true believers and often as leaders, will try to do damage in communities of faith and therefore we need to watch out and be on guard against such people. The patterns we observe with abusers are not unknown to God. He warns us about them in Scripture. One way to balance being on guard and on the defensive against potential abusers is to find and love ordinary saints. So much goodness can be found in God's humble people in the pews of every church. When we lose heart in the celebrity leaders of our generation, may we remember the thousands of living saints who are serving Jesus and living out his kingdom day by day. Knowing such people has helped save my faith when leaders have shattered it.

Additionally, although the uncovering of abuse feels like defeat and setback in faith terms, this is not the case. Jesus speaks of how God's work is to bring all things into the light (Luke 8:17). Revealing deeds of darkness is a work of the light, and it is a sign of God's kingdom coming. In the midst of supporting a sexual assault survivor last year, I found myself feeling low and overwhelmed by the oceans of pain and the weight of injustice suffered. A dear friend encouraged me: "The gift of prophecy in the church right now is calling these dark truths into the light, confronting this evil with the goodness and truth of the living God. Prophecy is less words of knowledge or encouraging preaching and more this work of justice calling a halt to leaders who abuse." I can picture where I was when she said it. We were standing in a British railway station about to travel in different directions after a time of fellowship. The uncovering of abuse is not defeat—it is the light shining in the darkness. The work of advocating for truth is prophetic.

My final thought as we ask, "Where is God when abuse is uncovered in the church? Is any of this God talk real? Can we ever really trust God?" is this: throw yourself on Jesus. Jesus shows us God with us in human flesh. Jesus suffered unspeakable horrors and shows us the love of God as real and good and true through his suffering. Cling to Jesus and read the words of Jesus. I found myself reading an entire Gospel in one sitting and the very words of Jesus ministering powerfully to me. Encountering Jesus is what I needed again and again. Only then could I begin to trust God when everything was shaken.

None of this needs to be thought through or done in a hurry. Take time. Don't rush. If God is God, he can handle our questions, fury, pain, and devastation. But I hope these thoughts will be helpful to you. Remember you are not alone—others have walked this path before and will walk it with you.

With love,
Amy

Gaslighting

Dear Jo,

I am writing to you from my kitchen table. I have a small vase of flowers cut from the garden in front of me. Simple pleasures bring such joy and beauty to ordinary life. I appreciate the grounding the flowers I have grown give me because the thoughts I want to share with you relate to a phenomenon that does the opposite.

It is hard for intelligent, gifted, or strong leaders to understand how gaslighting could possibly work. Surely a smart and capable person wouldn't be led to question their own perceptions of reality? Deep down I suspect I believed gaslighting would work only on people who struggled intellectually. What a fool I was, and how arrogant. It worked on me.

The term *gaslighting* comes from a classic movie in which an abusive husband chips away at his wife and convinces her that she is losing her mind and can't trust her own perceptions of reality.[1] For example, he dims the lights in their home and then denies that the lights have changed when she points it out.

In spiritual contexts, skillful gaslighters use a person's desire for piety against them. A person's desire to please God, or be humble, or be obedient to the Scriptures is used as a weapon. This might look like getting a whistleblower to second-guess them-selves by convincing them that they did not see what they say they saw and that they are a cynical and bad person to even entertain negative thoughts about a man of God. The spiritual danger of pride might be pointed out and attempts made to persuade the questioner that they are a proud person who is usurping the ac-countability structures of the organization by insisting on asking questions that are far above their station. They may be painted as a disloyal person for not siding with the leader when the leader was attacked in the spiritual battle. Or the whistleblower may be pressured to believe they are a gossip for verbalizing concerns to another person.

A Christian who has tried to cultivate an openness to feedback and who has a desire to repent if wrongdoing is brought to their attention may be particularly vulnerable here, since gaslighting is easily confused with learning from those in authority over us. This is profoundly disorienting because embracing the pain of cri-tique is crucial for genuine spiritual and personal growth. Mature Christians want to welcome the pruning that Jesus speaks of in

John 15. They may have worked hard to be people who don't fear confession and repentance, knowing that Jesus can be trusted. So when a trusted leader offers insights, it seems right and healthy to believe what they are saying and to have a penitent heart. The devastation of discovering that you should not have trusted a particular leader can bring about a brutal collapse of trust in people and even in God. This is part of the ripple effect of the mess and confusion that abuse brings into communities. I have found it helpful to name gaslighting, and I hope that reading this letter might alert you to this possibility before it happens.

I empathize with those who completely deconstruct all faith after an experience like this. We had a shower upstairs in our home that was the source of water leaking through the ceiling in the hallway below. Numerous fixes were undertaken, and the ceiling was repainted three times. Only when a builder took down all the tiles and took up the entire floor in the shower did we realize that the shower had never been properly sealed. A piece of unsealed wood had disintegrated over eleven years, and so if we hadn't started from scratch, that leak would never have been fixed. Deconstruction was necessary.

For me, deconstructing layers of deception and abuse was not the end. The rot needed to go, and there has been a significant season of lament and soul searching. The work to remove the toxic layers and false messages of spiritual leaders has taken time. There have been many days when I felt unable to trust Christians or even God. On some of those days, I found comfort that God-breathed Holy Scripture gives me words for my doubt and lament. God knew, even as the Holy Spirit inspired the writers of the Bible, that his people would need such words in times of trouble. Deconstruction of what was rotten and devastating was needed, but it was not the end of faith for me. God has proven faithful. I am slower to trust Christians now, and I am acutely tuned to power dynamics and false spiritual hierarchies. I question more and trust less. But I have hope in the person of Jesus, the love of the Father, and the presence of the Holy Spirit.

I have also realized that truth matters more profoundly than anything else in breaking free from gaslighting. While Pilate asked, "What is truth?" (John 18:38), Jesus said, "I am . . . the truth" (14:6). The light of the world, in whom there is no darkness, can by his Spirit "guide [us] into all the truth" (16:13). The one who said, "The truth will set you free" (8:32) can help us break free from the power of gaslighting. The value he placed on truth was both confronting and comforting to me. Everything is not a matter of perspective; there is such a thing as truth. Finding freedom from the tactics of gaslighters begins and ends with the power of truth. I needed truth from outside myself, a voice from outside my own head. I found that truth and heard that voice through reading the Gospel of John afresh.

I am slower to respond to inspiration or opportunity with unfettered faith, and I find I am now susceptible to the temptation to trust in the material security of assets in a way that didn't affect me before. I find I need to pray daily for a soft and trusting heart and to ask for help to respond in faith. But when I look at Jesus and see the "man of sorrows [who is] acquainted with grief" (Isa. 53:3 ESV), I realize that I know him more intimately. Recovering from religious gaslighting has given me a new union with the one who was despised and rejected by the religious authorities.

If you find yourself in the depths of disorienting, disillusioning gaslighting, know there is space for you to deconstruct what is rotten; there are words in the Scriptures to express lament, frustration, and doubt; and there is a truth outside yourself in the person and word of Jesus Christ. He can be trusted.

With very much love,
Amy

The Danger of Exceptionalism

Dear Jo,

As we reel from public revelations about leaders' moral wrong-doing, we face many serious questions. In fact, I believe one of the biggest apologetic questions of our age addresses whether the gospel really produces goodness, beauty, and truth in the lives of people and in the cultures they make around them. In other words, is the gospel good? Can it transform lives for the better?

I believe we are in a time when we need to take that question very seriously. That is a painful thing to do. There is serious work to be done to amend our hearts and practices so that we don't just have strong theoretical or doctrinal bases for what we are building but can point to embodied, incarnated, Jesus-centered communities that have a gospel culture of goodness, beauty, and truth.

A culture of goodness does not arise by accident. All too easily the churches and organizations we see around us have adopted toxic patterns of celebrity culture, exceptionalism, love of money, power grabs, cover-ups, gaslighting, sexual abuse, cancel culture, and fear. Meanwhile, the nations are crying out for justice, good-ness, beauty, and truth, and the church does not seem ready for this moment. In this letter, I hope to explore one tendency that leads us away from a gospel culture: exceptionalism.

Exceptionalism is the leadership approach that says verbally and nonverbally, "I am different / more special than you, so the rules don't apply to me in the same way they apply to you." There are tiers of importance, and the leaders at the top enjoy special privileges and indulge in behaviors that are not acceptable for people below them. Leaders are lavished with rewards and operate by different standards than everyone else.

The church has seen forms of exceptionalism before. Gnos-ticism held that there is secret spiritual knowledge that can be acquired by special individuals. The church had to fight this in the third and fourth centuries as a threat to the priesthood of all believers, the sufficiency of the cross of Christ to save anyone, and the Scriptures as a guide into all truth.

A second form of exceptionalism involved a new kind of priest caste in which leaders had the power to lead people into the pres-ence of God and were rewarded with material benefits for doing so. This was rejected during the Reformation when Luther, Calvin, Zwingli, and others sought to balance the power of the clergy, put a stop to their excesses and abuses, and emphasize the priesthood of all believers. Leaders cannot save us.

Exceptionalism can be detected where there's a sense of supe-riority over other Christians. The disciplines of the faith are for the little people, but once I reach the top, I am owed more ma-terial comforts and the indulgence of my stress being expressed in anger, mistreatment of staff, or actions that are clearly of poor Christian character.

Where you see signs of exceptionalism, be alert. If there are standards that apply to lower levels of staff and not to people higher up the chain of command, raise the red flag. Exceptionalism often occurs alongside other dysfunctions and abuses.

We also need to guard against exceptionalism in our own hearts. Ask yourself these questions as you grow in leadership and influence: Am I growing apart from those I lead? Am I seeking special treatment that Jesus never wanted or welcomed? In Mark 10:42–45, Jesus addresses this dilemma directly: "Jesus called them together and said, 'You know that those who are regarded as rulers of the Gentiles lord it over them, and their high officials exercise authority over them. Not so with you. Instead, whoever wants to become great among you must be your servant, and whoever wants to be first must be slave of all. For even the Son of Man did not come to be served, but to serve, and to give his life as a ransom for many.'"

As a leader who is sometimes in the spotlight, I have found it helpful to avoid exceptionalism by taking opportunities to serve in the background. This may be volunteering with children's or youth ministry or cooking and serving food and refreshments. It may be hosting refugees or serving those escaping domestic violence and other forms of abuse. Work that keeps me off the stage and gives me the chance to serve is a blessing.

Leaders need to actively seek out opportunities to follow the command of Jesus to serve and not be served. We can do this by working in the shadows for a time and choosing to prioritize unseen work in the same way we do for work that brings us public accolades.

With very much love,
Amy

Justice Takes a Long Time

Dear Jo,

I'm currently in the midst of advocating for people who were abused in their youth. It is a grueling process to move toward an independent investigation when a leader is powerful and high profile. One of the greatest blessings I experienced when I was in the eye of a different storm was the advice and encouragement of Dr. Diane Langberg. Langberg is a psychologist and author who has spent decades helping victims of sexual and spiritual abuse in religious settings. She generously answered questions and coached me and others on how to respond to the unfolding crisis we faced and helped us to use our voices for good.

Two particular instances stand out. At one point, I was stuck in a rut of hoping that senior leaders in the organization in question would wake up and change their posture once they received this or that piece of evidence. If only they heard this testimony or reflected on that statement they had made that was now demonstrably untrue, then surely they would apologize and decide to do the right thing. After all, these leaders were friends and colleagues who loved the Lord. As I was articulating this hope, Langberg stopped me, lowered her glasses, and focused her eyes on me. "Amy, stop. You must stop hoping."

She explained that I was paralyzed by the hope that people I loved would do the right thing. This was preventing me from moving forward and acting more decisively. She said that abusers and deceivers and their enablers weaponize this hope and thrive on it in Christian settings because it allows them to continue with their schemes. Her words to me, "Stop hoping," cut me to the heart. But she was absolutely right. This breakthrough moment helped me to stand more confidently for the oppressed and accept that things were far worse than I had feared in the organization I had trusted.

On another occasion, a dear friend was in a similar meeting with Langberg. He was expressing his fear that, as he started to believe there was a deception problem in the organization and not just in the person at the top who had been investigated and found to be an abuser, he was becoming cynical about fellow believers. Langberg stopped him as he poured out his heart and exclaimed, "Not nearly cynical enough!" Christians are taught to trust leaders and fellow believers and warned about the sin lurking in their own heart, the danger of gossip, and the problem of disloyalty. Their conscience is then weaponized against them, and their discernment is branded as cynical. The messaging is so strong that their own inner voice causes them to second-guess themselves.

Because of these dynamics—conditioning toward hope and a concern about cynicism—Christians can be peculiarly susceptible to abuse and slow to wake up to the deceptive and unhealthy patterns around them. This often means that the pursuit of justice is a longer haul than it should be. A conversation with Rachael Denhollander helped me to realize this. She warned me, "Justice takes far longer than you think it will." I have remembered those words as I have continued to advocate for others in their suffering in various settings. We need to be prepared for justice to take longer than it should. The dynamics in Christian communities often make it hard for people to see and believe something horrifying that flies in the face of everything they have been conditioned to expect.

Having this awareness and a willingness to take up a cause that will not in all likelihood resolve quickly has helped me so much.

Justice takes far longer than you think it will. If you find yourself entangled in a complex or toxic situation, I pray that the Lord will renew your strength and give you the courage to persist.

With love,
Amy

PART 6

Finding Hope
in
Dark Times

Anxiety

Dear Jo,

One of the things most Christian leaders will face at some point is a period of anxiety, characterized as a pervasive feeling that things are not okay. It is possible to have a loving support structure of family, friends, community, and team yet deep down still feel bereft and anxious.

High-functioning anxiety can mean that outwardly we look fine. We exhibit attention to detail and social confidence and achieve outstanding results. But inside anxiety gnaws away and drives us to work harder, to deliver the results we feel we need to, and to make it over the next hurdle in the hope that when we get there we will feel better. But we never seem to make it to the end of the list or reach the day when there are no more worries.

Anxiety can also express itself as hypervigilance. We wait for the sky to fall while constantly working to prevent our fears from happening. The drive to do enough, navigate all the pitfalls, and keep pushing forward can be crippling.

Anxiety might show up as panic. I first experienced something close to panic in an MRI machine after a back injury. I was sweating and trying not to shake inside the claustrophobic tube, willing myself not to press the button that alerts the staff to get you out. I recited psalms and hymns, but it was really difficult.

As a perfectionist, I have lived my life working hard and overpreparing for situations so that whatever happened I would be okay. I have been in a lot of high-adrenaline situations around the world, addressing large audiences and taking questions, speaking in high-profile political settings, smuggling Bibles or doing ministry events in countries where it is illegal to do so, and ministering among gang members. I believed that fear was a luxury I could not entertain. In dangerous situations, I found God or another motivator within so that I could feel I was operating in faith and courage.

After a traumatic experience in my forties, my tactics didn't work anymore. I would be struck by a panic attack out of the blue. One time I was swimming in the ocean with my husband and children. Panic hit me, and I gasped for breath. I thought I was having a heart attack. I would have drowned if my husband hadn't gotten ahold of me and helped me back to shore.

At other times, low-level anxiety bubbled away, and I could feel every sinew of my body surging with cortisol. On the darkest days, I prayed for oblivion—just to feel relief. Anxiety is like an unabating nausea.

During an anxious time, we are vulnerable. It is worth prioritizing getting help from established mental health practitioners. I have been profoundly helped by therapy. It is not something to be ashamed of. Admitting you need an outside perspective is an act of courage. One of the things that helped me the most was thinking about how much I love my children and how I would do anything I could to alleviate their suffering or fears. When my therapist asked me whether I could extend the same kindness to myself and envision God offering me that kind of love, something within me broke. I experienced the deep truth that love casts out fear. Alongside therapy over a protracted period, I received a flow of divine love that tended to my anxious soul.

As leaders, we grow in competence and confidence and in many other glorious ways through the years. But I needed to learn how to receive love in a new way in order to heal from anxiety. And I needed to learn how to extend kindness to myself, to change the tone and content of my inner dialogue. The compassion I could easily offer those I cared for or served needed to be turned within.

We can also turn to the Lord and receive mercy, strength, and help from him. Step one is admitting we need support. Leaders strongly tend toward self-reliance. We may see ourselves as the one others look to, the person who has solutions and not problems. But none of us is ever beyond looking to God as our helper and deliverer. When anxiety stalks, call on the name of the Lord. In fact, I have found it helpful to study the names of the Lord in the Old Testament. In ancient cultures, a name signified something about a person, and in the Bible, God is revealed through many beautiful names. God is El-Roi, the God who sees, revealed to Hagar in the desert in her desperate need (Gen. 16:13). God is El-Shaddai, the Lord Almighty who tenderly delivers those who look to him (Gen. 17:1; 35:11). God is Jehovah Rophe, the God who heals (Exod. 15:26). When I focus on who God is, look to him, lean on him, I can take my eyes off my thoughts and worries and circumstances and see the one who can encourage and deliver me.

In Luke 12, Jesus addresses his disciples in a section of teaching on worry and anxiety. "Then Jesus said to his disciples: 'Therefore I tell you, do not worry about your life, what you will eat; or about your body, what you will wear. For life is more than food, and the body more than clothes'" (vv. 22–23). It struck me that as a young, pioneering leader, I did not worry about these things, but living in a materialistic, consumer age, we can get sucked into this way of thinking. A materialistic worldview operates on a scarcity mindset. There is a limited amount of resources, and so I need to acquire them to protect myself and my family. Leading well in the way of Jesus means actively resisting the impetus to worry about clothes and food and the acquisition of assets. Living for a different kingdom means trusting that "your Father knows that you need them" (v. 30). We are released from anxiety and worry as we resist the power of consumerism and mass consumption around us and the mentality of acquisition and owning more and more and more. My relationships with wealthy secular friends confirm the reality that wealth does not deliver people from anxiety or worry.

If we can find a secure base in our relationship with Christ, then we will be released from so many of the worries of this life and will be able to lead with a freedom and security that are rare and beautiful. Jesus sums up his teaching by saying, "Do not be afraid, little flock, for your Father has been pleased to give you the kingdom" (Luke 12:32). We can revel in being his little flock and having a relationship of attachment, tenderness, affection, and intimacy. Leaders who have received the kingdom are not driven by acquisition, power, celebrity, the need to make an impact, or a sense of importance. In the kingdom, small is precious, small is good—a very small amount of yeast can have a huge effect for good (see Luke 13:21–22). If we think along the lines of the empires and power structures of this world, we will build churches and organizations that seek impressive influence. Kingdom influence is subtle and may seem small or unimpressive, but to Jesus being his little flock matters greatly. And it is a key to living free from fear.

When anxiety strikes, you are not alone. Jesus anticipated that his disciples would experience fear and worry. If you need to seek professional guidance, don't be ashamed to do so. And when you need help from heaven, turn to God and ask for it, revel in being part of his little flock, and receive again the upside-down kingdom that the Father is pleased to give you.

With love,
Amy

Trauma

Dear Jo,

As I think about you this evening, I am sitting in Denmark, where the sunshine, natural beauty, and expanse of sky make the world feel like a good and safe place. But I find myself reflecting on the contrast between the goodness, beauty, and truth of God's creation and the pain and trauma that life will throw at us as we live, lead, and work. Even if you don't experience trauma yourself, as a leader you will certainly live with, love, and lead those who do. Supporting a traumatized person can be a steep learning curve. I experienced this initially when supporting my husband through complex post-traumatic stress as a result of abuse and trauma he suffered in childhood.

I used to think of the word *trauma* as referring to a physical injury or a surgery required after injury. Now I know that trauma is less about what happened to you and more about what happens inside of you as a result of what happened to you.[1] Trauma is less about the immediate impact of a devastating event and more about the long-term impact on the whole person. Trauma is an embodied thing. It goes way beyond thoughts, feelings, or even psychology. Trauma is *in* the body, stored in our hormonal and musculature pathways. Trauma can evoke two extremes of emotional response: feeling overwhelmed or feeling numb. When the body and the nervous system are overwhelmed, this impacts our capacity to cope with day-to-day challenges, while numbing can be a way of coping with stress and surviving in daily life.

I have learned that dissociation, overachieving, floods of emotion, fight, flight, freeze, and fawn are among the many trauma survival mechanisms. We even see them in the pages of Scripture. The prophet Elijah, for example, experienced such despair that he could not eat and wanted to die (1 Kings 19:1–9). Such people were not written off by God. Ultimately, the love of God was shown to our world through the trauma of his Son as he died by crucifixion.

There are endless redemptive possibilities for trauma survivors in the flow of faith, and the powers exhibited by human beings who overcome trauma and go on to thrive are well documented in scientific literature. Hypervigilance, strong intuition, empathy, outside-the-box thinking, and functionality in highly stressful, complex situations are just some of the many powers that those who have survived trauma are likely to have. "Post-traumatic growth" is the term used by trauma specialists to talk of these possible benefits, including enhanced personal relationships and spiritual understanding.[2] A person who has overcome horror and survived to build a beautiful life may still suffer from brain fog, triggers, panic, and moments of feeling overwhelmed, but their strength and dignity are stunning to behold.

I encourage you today to have empathy for anyone in your life who has survived trauma—even if their dissociative or forgetful habits seem annoying. Embrace the creative and empathic genius that follows in the wake of those who have come through traumatic experiences. And be a person who stays the course and consistently shows up to support teammates, family members, and colleagues who walk the trauma path. Remember that at the center of the Christian faith is a Savior, God in the flesh, who was traumatized by abuse, an unjust trial, nakedness, whipping, betrayal by those he loved, and crucifixion. We follow a traumatized Savior, and it is through his broken body that redemption and love are offered to this world.

Don't write off people who have endured the unspeakable. Trauma survivors are heroic figures. Yes, they will need support and empathy and love. But the world and the church need their talents, insights, creativity, empathy, and energy more than ever. If we are going to serve and reach a generation, we need to create safe places for trauma survivors to heal, thrive, and flourish.

And if you experience some degree of trauma yourself, don't minimize it or ignore it, thinking others have suffered worse. Pay attention to your need, and get the help you require for yourself and for the sake of those around you and those you lead. Trauma need not write you off or leave you on the scrap heap. There is hope. There is a future. You are loved.

With love,
Amy

When You Can't Pray

Dear Jo,

There may be times in life when you just can't pray. I have certainly found this to be the case. When I have felt like the sky is falling, at times it has thrown me into deeper prayer and connection with God, as I recognized my need for him. At other times, prayer has been a real struggle.

A long time ago, I went through a dark and painful time of difficulty conceiving a child. It all began with a dramatic collapse in the street in my twenties. One minute I was fine, and the next I had fallen to the ground unconscious. An ambulance was called and drove me to the nearest hospital. I was away from home on work, and my husband had to make life-and-death decisions from a distance.

It turned out I had a ruptured ovarian cyst. The pain was so excruciating that I had blacked out. The operation was a success, but after an additional diagnosis of endometriosis, the doctor advised us to get on with trying to have a baby.

In the following three years, I continued to work, speak, write, travel, and help my husband lead the churches we were a part of. We went through bouts of hope and despair as long waits were punctuated by two miscarriages, one of which happened at the largest Christian youth festival in the United Kingdom as I was about to answer apologetics questions for ten thousand young people. The shock, devastation, indignity, and grief for a life lost are hard to put into words. There is a peculiar sorrow in carrying death inside your womb, which is meant for life. The longed-for child is no more, but they are still inside your body.

Some days I prayed desperately, clinging to Scripture. But other weeks I was frozen, unable to pray. I found myself doubting at a fundamental level whether God loved me. Deep down I felt the sadness and loss crushing any remaining vestige of trust in God. I was a preacher, a theologian, an evangelist, a writer, a pastor's wife, a leader with access to political and other high-power settings for God, but I couldn't pray or trust him myself. What a failure I was.

At this point, a more mature Christian mentioned to me that he rarely prayed spontaneously. He shared that as he grew in the Christian life, he had found the effort needed to reinvent the prayer wheel with fluent speeches to be exhausting and disheartening. He told me that he daily prayed the psalms and the prayers of the church—liturgy—and that other more personal or immediate prayers flowed from that.

Although I grew up Anglican, we were relatively low church. I loved the short liturgical parts of the service—the confession, absolution, creeds, and Eucharistic prayers. The words were so familiar, washing over me every week. I knew liturgy to be good, beautiful, and true in community, but I had never thought to practice private prayer using liturgy or contemplation of Scripture. Bible reading and prayer had been separate disciplines for me in a daily quiet time.

In the darkest season of my life to that point, I learned to pray all over again by echoing the prayers of those who have gone before us. Their words carried me through and became a part of my daily life.

"Lighten our darkness we beseech thee, O Lord, and by thy great mercy defend us from all perils and dangers of this night. For the love of thine only Son our Savior Jesus Christ. Amen."[1] In the night when darkness and worry pressed in, this prayer soon came easily to mind. Then when our twin boys were born nearly four years after my operation, I was able to pray this over them in the watches of the night. And then throughout their and their younger brother's childhoods, we prayed the Lord's Prayer and this prayer together every evening. Before they could read a word, they were fluent in these prayers.

I am still discovering a wealth of faithful collects and scriptural prayers to keep me praying when all else fails. Perhaps like me you might find them to be a lifeline of faith. These prayers of the church also have a way of forming us in depth and truth, reminding us that prayer is less about self-realization or verbal fluency and more about becoming truly and deeply connected to the eternal God himself.

Maybe the prayers of the church will sustain you too through the long years of a life of faith and through the dark valleys that any life journey will pass through. Don't worry when your own words fail. There's more to prayer than individual eloquence, creativity, or fervor. Seek the wells of grace to drink from in the Scriptures and in the liturgy of faithful churches.

With my love,
Amy

Consolation

Dear Jo,

Increasingly when discouragement or despair creeps up on me, one phrase comes to mind in prayer: "God our consolation." In the midst of pressure, sadness, and anxiety, this phrase has reminded me of the boundless love of God for me when I have most needed it.

Consolation is an old-fashioned word. When I was growing up, my much-loved German grandmother, Oma, always gave not only a gift to the child whose birthday it was but also a small amount of money to the others. She called it the "consolation prize." It was a reminder that each child was seen and loved, celebrated and remembered, including when the focus was rightly on one of the other children.

I never had any doubt that I mattered to her. Sometimes her love was a bit overwhelming. As a child, I once commented that I liked kiwifruit. For the next few years, every time I saw her she had bags full of kiwis that could not possibly be consumed by one person.

My oma stands out in my life as a woman who loved with extravagant joy. She had suffered unimaginably during and after World War II, but love, music, beauty, and joy poured out of her, so much so that more than twenty-five years after her death, I still think of her most days. As lovely as her gifts were, *she* was the consolation, and it was her unwavering love that has been a basis for my own sense of personhood.

For followers of Jesus, it is God himself—his love, his presence, his beauty, his goodness—that is the consolation. The psalmist reminds us that God "is close to the brokenhearted and saves those who are crushed in spirit" (Ps. 34:18). In times of sadness, disappointment, lament, and concern, the Lord is my consolation—not finally getting to the end of the to-do list, not vindication in human terms when I have been harmed, not acknowledgment or praise from people when I think my work deserves it. Closeness to him, the unshakeable knowledge of being loved by him, the deep certainty of shalom that all is well because of him—this is the deepest consolation any of us can experience.

Time and time again I have found this to be the case, but in desperate times it is not enough to know this in theory. It needs to be felt. A few practical things have been helpful for me in this regard. Meditation on the Scriptures, getting outside to pray in a place of beauty, asking a friend to pray for me, and sitting by an open fire and taking time to focus on Christ have proven meaningful. Looking backward or probing within won't lift the load or comfort the heart, but naming the pain in the presence of God and giving it to him will.

Older, wiser Christians might be able to help us on our journey of faith, having walked a similar path before us. I have found it invaluable to know leaders in their seventies and older and to sit with them in the presence of the Lord, to listen to their thoughts and experiences, to draw encouragement from the God who is faithful through the generations. The active presence of the living God is a reality. He gives rest and strength and pours his love "into our hearts through the Holy Spirit" (Rom. 5:5) over and over. This is a solid expectation in the Christian life.

As the pressures mount and the stakes get bigger, we need to walk and live in the consolation of the Lord more and more. Seek his love and consolation more each year, not less.

With love,
Amy

Reframing Forgiveness

Dear Jo,

A while ago I slipped into a pew in one of Britain's most beautiful cathedrals at dusk for evensong. I got chills when the choir sang the words of Mary's Magnificat: "He hath put down the mighty from their seats and exalted them of low degree."

I had spent that day sitting in the public gallery of a courtroom supporting someone who was giving evidence in a criminal trial concerning childhood abuse. Mary's words of hope on behalf of the poor, the humble, and the powerless felt especially meaningful that evening. Several weeks later I remembered her words again when I sat in a basement room with another woman giving testimony to investigators about the violent sexual assault she had endured at the hands of a teacher who lectured at the institution where she worked.

This letter is adapted from a 2023 talk given at the UK Parliament's National Prayer Breakfast.

In our individual lives and in this cultural moment, it feels like there is so much loss and harm, and so our awareness of injustice is heightened. Justice movements recognize the potency of the harm inflicted on a human being when wrong is done. We are a generation rightly crying out for justice. But that means that when we really think about harm and trauma, the word *forgiveness* might make us flinch. It can sound a lot like *minimizing* the harm.

The former archbishop of Cape Town, Desmond Tutu, held his post during the apartheid era in South Africa, winning a Nobel Peace Prize in 1984 for his opposition to the brutal regime. He led the country's Truth and Reconciliation Commission after the election of Nelson Mandela in 1994 and was frequently seen crying during the hearings as victims faced and challenged their torturers, telling their stories and reliving the atrocities. The central purpose of the commission was to promote reconciliation and forgiveness among perpetrators and victims of apartheid through the full disclosure of truth. Tutu wrote, "Forgiving is not forgetting; it's actually remembering—remembering and not using your right to hit back. It's a second chance for a new beginning. And the remembering part is particularly important. Especially if you don't want to repeat what happened."[1] In other words, forgiveness and justice should not be mutually exclusive.

But in our quest for justice, is it possible that we have lost the art of forgiveness? It feels like something more akin to hatred and a lack of tolerance is all around us. From the impetus to punish a person whose ideas or behavior we disagree with, to lobbying to get a person fired or banned from public life, a lack of grace thrives. High-profile individuals have had to endure campaigns of harassment and intimidation in the name of justice. People involved in public life often experience the volatile and ominous nature of interacting online and in other settings. But adults are not alone in this experience. Many school children and teenagers are now fearful to express their thoughts lest they find themselves attacked. Once a person is singled out, it seems there is no hope for public forgiveness, repentance, and changed lives. Accountability is everything, and redemption feels impossible.

Driving this is a passion for justice and a stark refusal to roll over and accept harm. There is a rejection of the unqualified relativism of postmodernism. After all, something matters in absolute terms if injustice matters. Individuals matter, and so culture matters, and so society matters. For so long, people in positions of power have been able to act with impunity, but now there is a manifest desire (albeit imperfectly) to hold powerful figures to account in some way.

I believe that the Christian faith has something profound to say to us in this cultural moment as well as some important questions to pose.

First, it is worth considering why we feel outrage at the suffering in the world or at perceived injustices at all. If this material world of biology, physics, and chemistry is all there is, why should we experience disgust and fury at the exploitation of human beings who are merely the product of a random process of chance and a contest for the survival of the fittest? Why should we matter if we are just here by chance? Doesn't our rage at injustice tell us something about who we are?

Of course, materialists and agnostics, as well as Christians, experience anger and outrage in the face of injustice and the suffering of others. But my question is, What can account for that anger? If human beings are created in the image of God, that is true whether an individual believes it or not. Life is sacred, and we have different ways of seeing this and knowing it to be true. One Old Testament poet claims that God has "set eternity in the human heart" (Eccles. 3:11). Our human rage at injustice points beyond itself to the sacredness of life and that possibility of eternity in our hearts—the possibility that we are infinitely precious, unimaginably loved by our Creator, image bearers of the divine.

Second, if our culture holds out little possibility of redemption and forgiveness is seen as moral weakness, is this what we want? Redemption is one of the grand themes in the literature and art of many civilizations, and it matters deeply to us as human beings. Forgiveness and redemption are being lost to a cold cruelty that is reminiscent of authoritarian regimes of the past. Perhaps some in our generation have lost personal contact with such systems of the past. At forty-seven, I am old enough to remember conversations with my grandparents who escaped from East Germany to Britain to avoid being taken by the Soviets to Siberia. My father, just a small child then, is here today. They observed and lived under the cruelty of totalitarian political systems, both right wing and left. As human beings, we are wired for redemption, and so the possibility of forgiveness matters greatly.

So the big question is this: Is there such a thing as forgiveness that does not minimize harm or dehumanize those who have suffered horror?

I want to suggest that genuine faith that is shaped by the historic person of Jesus Christ has something truly profound to offer us. The instinct in culture that harm matters so profoundly that a person must pay and even die some kind of social or professional death for their transgression points beyond itself to the story that has given meaning to millions around the world. Jesus of Nazareth, as God incarnate, God in the flesh, willingly died by crucifixion at the hands of the Romans. His death is described in the New Testament as a ransom, an offering, and a sacrifice. He paid a price for the transgressions of the world. And that means forgiveness can be real. The price we all intuitively sense must be paid for harm was actually paid by Jesus.

Forgiveness may be rejected by some as a weakness that denies the seriousness of wrongdoing. But Christian forgiveness does not say the thing that happened to us didn't hurt, it wasn't wrong, or it didn't matter. Forgiveness means that the incident did hurt, it was wrong, and it does matter. Since every human being has been made in the image of God, our suffering matters profoundly. But we have the power to forgive, to release a person from our vengeance, because we trust that justice will ultimately be done. We can support civil justice in this life, and we can trust that there will be eternal justice in the hands of God. Transgression and harm will be judged by a higher authority than us. If any of us truly repents and owns our wrongdoing, we can be forgiven in an ultimate sense because someone *has* paid for our transgressions. The death of the Son of God points to the extraordinary cost and the vast value placed on each one of us by a loving God. Christian forgiveness underlines the seriousness of the harm that has occurred because forgiving it requires the suffering and death of God. This is not cheap.

In practical terms, I want to suggest that the concept of Christian forgiveness is a gift to any culture. And it is available to all of us. Forgiveness and redemption are possible, *and* outrage at injustice has a foundation in reality. The Christian message acknowledges that wrongdoing is real and that there is real justice to be done. It challenges us to admit that all of us are flawed in some way and need forgiveness.

The late queen Elizabeth II noted in her 2016 Christmas broadcast, "Forgiveness lies at the heart of the Christian faith. It can heal broken families, it can restore friendships, and it can reconcile divided communities. It is in forgiveness that we feel the power of God's love."[2]

My friend Ben Kwashi has served as the archbishop of Jos in Plateau State, Nigeria, for many years. He has survived three assassination attempts, a brutal assault on his wife, Gloria, and the burning of his home. These acts drove them both to their knees—to forgive and to find the strength to carry on serving the people of their community. The Kwashis have adopted eighty-five orphans and live in a place of incredible tension with outstanding joy and peace. They live in a flow of forgiveness that builds schools and trains leaders to love across difference. They build churches that serve communities and lead to friendships across divides. Forgiveness in action is beautiful and compelling, and it helps rebuild a broken world.

The Christian offer of forgiveness is for everyone—to receive it and to be empowered to give it. Being offered forgiveness I don't deserve that does not minimize the harm I have caused and yet affirms my belovedness is the heart of God's forgiveness in Christ. Through the ages, this forgiveness has had the power to change the trajectory of a life. It turns a person around and sets them on a path of goodness, beauty, and truth instead of wrongdoing. Forgiveness also had the power to liberate me from ongoing harm when I was the victim. It liberated me from the burden of accomplishing vengeance—a feat beyond me—and freed me to live without bitterness and in peace.

The power to forgive may just be the greatest gift the Christian story can offer our age. The *Truth and Reconciliation Commission of South Africa Report* notes:

We have been privileged to help to heal a wounded people, though we ourselves have been, in Henri Nouwen's profound and felicitous phrase, "wounded healers." When we look around us at some of the conflict areas of the world, it becomes increasingly clear that there is not much of a future for them without forgiveness, without reconciliation. God has blessed us richly so that we might be a blessing to others. Quite improbably, we as South Africans have become a beacon of hope to others locked in deadly conflict that peace, that a just resolution, is possible. If it could happen in South Africa, then it can certainly happen anywhere else. Such is the exquisite divine sense of humor.[3]

I know this letter is longer than usual, but I hope you found these thoughts meaningful.

With very much love,
Amy

PART 7

Navigating Friendship

Hold On to Faithful Friends

Dear Jo,

As I think about you, with your work and ministry leadership mostly ahead of you, I'm reminded of the fateful advice a wise, older leader gave to my husband and me about friendship when we were training for ministry. He said, "Be very careful about having friends in the churches you lead." He quoted John 2:24: "Jesus would not entrust himself to them, for he knew all people."

I remember thinking, *No, it won't be like that for us.*

The truth is that working with close friends on projects and business ventures and in churches and organizations has been a huge source of joy and encouragement. But it is also true that the greatest anguish and pain in my work and ministry have come from hurts inflicted by people I trusted and counted as friends. The psalmist conveys the pain of lost friendships when he speaks of people "with whom I once enjoyed sweet fellowship at the house of God as we walked about among the worshipers" (Ps. 55:14).

Jesus knows the pain of betrayal. In fact, the ending of the Gospel of John explores how the resurrected Jesus interacts with Peter after he has publicly denied him. I thought about this a great deal when I was hurting over conflict in a church I loved and processing the actions of people I considered friends. Peter was one of the twelve disciples, and he denied Jesus. He completely and utterly failed in standing up for his beliefs and his community of closest friends. He turned away from Jesus as he went to his death. All the Gospels are honest about it. The episode is not whitewashed or removed from the history of the church or the Bible as an embarrassing secret. Failure, betrayal, and loss are expected parts of what it means to lead in God's church, according to the New Testament. Yet today in the church in the West, betrayal by friends feels like a dirty secret—a failure on our part that must be hidden.

I have worried as a leader that experiencing a breach with friends means that I am a failure as a person. But the Scriptures anticipate it for Christian leaders. Even Paul had a falling out with Barnabas over Mark. I think you will experience pain in close ministry relationships. I certainly have. If you do, remember this letter. You are not alone.

I can't protect you from the pain. No one can. Our minister's warning couldn't stop the trials from happening. But in retrospect, his warning offered a strange comfort. We realized we were not the only ones to experience failed friendships. We remembered that this kind of thing happens in the biblical story and that leaders can expect to face it. So when friendships go wrong, remember you are loved, you are not alone, and you are not weird.

Is there any hope? Yes! Invest in and hold on to faithful friends. Don't become so busy and important that you stop giving time to true, old friendships. And continue to make new friends. Prioritize your friend relationships with time, energy, commitment, creativity, and generosity. In my experience, God has new people for us in each decade. Don't build your relational life on too few friends, and resist the temptation to invest in relationships that are purely geographical or that are expedient for the task you have at hand. Invest in a range of friendships. If you are married, this is equally true. Don't retreat into the bubble of that one significant relationship. Keep investing in and loving your friends.

If you feel brokenhearted over a lost friendship, that shows something good about who you are. You love, you care, you live as if people matter. Time is a healer; the pain won't always hurt as much as it does at first.

Jesus's words about loving, forgiving, and blessing our enemies apply to former friends. Practice praying for them. Practice forgiveness in the sense that you release them from your own vengeance and condemnation and trust them to God. Doing this means you can get to the point of not flinching when you hear their names.

Also remember that healthy boundaries are not the same as unforgiveness. Sometimes you need to accept that a close connection is over and separation is necessary.

I pray that you will know the joy of lifelong, faithful friends. And I pray that when friendships fail, Jesus will carry you through, tend to your wounds, and help you forgive those who now feel like enemies.

With love,
Amy

Jealousy and Rivalry

Dear Jo,

One of the dynamics that can really hurt in leadership is when you find yourself on the receiving end of jealousy or rivalry. Sometimes onlookers will comment that imitation is the greatest form of flattery. But this is not the case if someone begins to try to replicate and ultimately replace you.

The truth is that we are all uniquely made in the image of God, so the minute I try to assume somebody else's gifts, position, mannerisms, style, or message, I am stepping out of who God made me to be. I'm no longer walking in step with the Spirit and the legacy of my own walk with God; I am imitating and even potentially usurping somebody else. It hurts all the more if someone we have sought to help or mentor attempts to do this. In fact, if we experience this, it may even dissuade us from helping younger people find their bearings. Regardless of whether our rival succeeds or fails in their quest to displace us and take something we have built and cherished, the experience can be bruising, even devastating.

I have experienced both. An attempt to push me out of things I led ultimately failed when the person's lack of substance within the field and immaturity became clear. It was still a huge shock to hear accounts of the campaign against me that had occurred, from outright imitation to subtle digs. Ultimately, in that instance my team resisted and brought to light what had happened. In a different setting, I was not so fortunate. A small group of people was determined to take over the leadership of something that had grown exponentially. I had to choose between fighting or letting go of something very precious. I knew at a certain point that if I fought for ownership and my own leadership, the team and the ministry I had helped to build would be destroyed. And so I withdrew, and ostensibly the rival won.

Both experiences brought pain into my life and caused me to question my leadership at the deepest level. Unfortunately, my experiences were not unique. I know that many leaders have faced similar situations on small and large scales. Rivalry is even a theme in Scripture. Hannah faced the rivalry of her husband's second wife, who bore him many children and intentionally provoked her infertile rival to the point of tears (1 Sam. 1:7). Jacob and Esau were rivals for their father's blessing (Gen. 27). In the New Testament, Paul addresses rivalry in the church in 1 Corinthians 4:6 and 2 Corinthians 12:20. Rivalry is profoundly painful to experience, and it doesn't seem possible to avoid.

So how do we manage others' jealousy and rivalry when we excel?

Rooting our core sense of identity in God helps enormously. That means when I am showered with praise for an achievement or breakthrough, it does not define me; the success is external to me. I can mark it and celebrate it, but I do not live and die by it. Equally, when I am attacked, my role or work does not define me, and so I can mourn the disappointment and lament the experience, but they are outside me. I am not destroyed by them.

How does this work day to day? Rooting my core sense of identity in God is a lifelong journey and involves daily prayer and Scripture reading that strengthen my connection with God. When I am connected to God, his love is poured out into my heart and my relationship with God as Father is strengthened—whether professional success or failure comes.

When you need to handle a rival, go forward in love and empathy. A person who is seeking to replace you does not have a solid sense of who they are or are meant to be. Approaching them with empathy helps in the process of forgiving the hurt. Understanding the dynamics of what is happening may empower you to challenge the rival in time, before significant damage has been done, and to request that they focus their energies and talents elsewhere.

If you realize the damage too late, there is comfort to be found in knowing you are not alone. You may feel discarded, and the sting of failure will hurt, but remember that Hannah's tears before God, due in part to her suffering at the hands of her rival, became the foundation for her breakthrough. Ultimately, this experience can strengthen you as a leader and prepare you for your next steps. You may more easily detect a rival in other settings and be ready to stand by leaders when similar patterns unfold. All is not lost. The gifts and skills that made someone seek to imitate or usurp you are still there, but now you have another string to wisdom's bow in your hand.

With very much love,
Amy

LETTER 32

When Friendships Become Transactional

Dear Jo,
An older Christian leader once told me, "From your forties onward, you make fewer friends in each decade than the one before.

Nurture your friendships and value the new connections you make as you get older."

A friend is a person with whom you share a bond. There is a deep knowing that you are there for each other, a knowing that transcends class, background, sex, race, and age. A friend says, "I see you, I get you, I love you."

Some relationships are proximity based, and when one party moves away, the friendship largely evaporates. Other friendships prove to be lifelong. It's okay when a friendship fades. Some plants are annuals that flower for a season and die, while others are perennials that last for generations. Both have value and beauty. But with a friendship, you are unlikely to know whether it's an annual or a perennial at any given time. Even if you did know, should it change how you treat the person in the moment? Would you walk away if you knew the friendship was just for a season? If you did, your ecosystem would be out of balance, and you would miss out on so much beauty and life.

Perhaps it is a self-protective instinct fueled by a good dose of hindsight that makes us wish we had given less and loved more cautiously when a friendship fades or disappears. But that approach cheapens relationships and diminishes ourselves and the other person.

There is a difference between a friendship that blossoms and then dies naturally and a relationship that is discarded after one person uses another transactionally under the guise of friendship. I realized a while ago that a person I had considered a dear friend had harvested my social network and used those connections to build their career. Some of those connections were then discarded when wealthier or more powerful connections came about. I too was slowly but eventually left behind in their pursuit of greater things.

This made me reflect on true friendship, what it means to nurture friendships, and how important it is to maintain friendships with people from every decade and stage of our lives. When the demands of leadership, work, and ministry press in, friendships can tend to be sacrificed on the altar of vision and productivity. The time, selflessness, and effort required to maintain a friendship (especially if we don't live in the same city) slip down the list of priorities.

But friendship is a key theme in the New Testament. As believers, we are called "friends of God," (John 15:13–15) and Jesus's ministry modeled spending time with a close circle of friends—the Twelve—and a wider circle of friends, the Seventy-Two (Luke 10:1–17).

Nurturing friendships is a crucial part of a healthy spiritual life, demonstrating that we value people over projects, not just in theory but in reality. In our triumphs, celebrations, and successes, life is all the sweeter when we have friends to share in the joy. Friendships can also sustain us when we stumble or life's circumstances beat us down. Friends who pray for us, stand with us, support us in practical ways, listen to our deepest thoughts, and faithfully keep on loving us, come what may, are worth their weight in gold. Friends who know what we're feeling because they know our backstory and have walked with us for years are irreplaceable.

So send a card, write a note, pick up the phone, and reach out. Meet up, listen, share, and pray. Don't treat friendship like a commodity; show up for people. Very few things will turn out to be as important in the long run as the friendships you nurtured.

As you grow in leadership and gain power or influence, your usefulness will attract people, and it will become more difficult to find true friends. If like me you have felt used, maneuvered, or leveraged at times, give thanks for the friendships you have in which this is not the case. Learn from what went wrong, and become more discerning as you meet people. Only recently did I realize that my approach to friendship had been shaped by a sense that all Christians are my family and so have access to me. I did not exercise caution when it came to Christians. I trusted without discernment. I paid a price for this. The answer is not to trust no one but to practice healthy caution. Take time to discern the character and compatibility of new friends, and keep delighting and investing in the friendships that have stood the test of time.

With very much love,
Amy

PART 8

Leading Like Jesus

Why Love Matters

Dear Jo,

Today I received two messages from leaders checking in with me to see if I was okay. One had a specific concern for me and felt prompted to write with an offer of help; the other wrote to encourage me. The impact for me was so much greater than the sum of the parts. The words mattered, but the thing that made the difference was love.

Love matters greatly in leadership. We can look at some situations and see how obvious this is. Loveless evangelism is always counterproductive. Evangelism that is technically proficient, intellectually accurate, or even impactful but ultimately loveless will not bear any fruit. In the same way, pastoring that is administratively efficient, theologically correct, or practically consistent but impersonal and lacking in love will not heal wounded hearts or deeply disciple God's people. Loveless parenting may raise children who are physically cared for and outwardly compliant, but it will not yield an emotionally healthy or connected family.

Jesus's statement in John 13:34, "As I have loved you, so you must love one another," is a manifesto for our leadership, work, life, and service. The "as . . . so" construction in Jesus's teaching gives us insight into how we are to love. In the life of Jesus, love looks like self-sacrifice, not self-realization. The way of Jesus is self-giving love.

Our faith is only as good as our love; without love, all our accomplishments, efforts, and breakthroughs are just noise. This runs counter to what culture values the most: power, fame, money, and respect.

In practical terms, love in the life of Jesus looks like time with the Father, time with the disciples, time with the poor and others whom society deemed inconsequential. Jesus's love is not a nice theory, nor is his love exercised at a distance. His love is particular, personal, granular, specific, and hands-on. By contrast, the disciples wanted greatness—and even had disputes and arguments over who was the greatest and who would get to sit where. The competitiveness, insecurity, self-centeredness, desire for prestige, and obsession with positional authority that are so familiar to us were exactly what they sought. But Jesus showed them and taught them that going after power is the antithesis of love.

Our culture is dominated by power—and it is making us disillusioned, anxious, and miserable. This generation needs a revolution of love.

Love compelled Jesus to empty himself of his power, his entitlement, and his privilege. The Greek word for self-emptying is *kenosis*. Jesus, who receives eternal glory and worship and is seated in authority and in loving harmony with the Father and the Spirit, entered this world in obscurity. He was the son of an unmarried teenage girl, a refugee on the move, a member of a people oppressed and living under Roman occupation. Jesus was born into a family shaped by trauma and weakness. That is how we are to lead and love—in weakness and fragility on human terms but full of the glorious love of God burning in our hearts.

Is love a missing part of your leadership? Have you gotten caught up in the tasks and responsibilities of your position? Is it time to recenter love as the priority that shapes and empowers your work?

When people see loving leadership, it changes them. May you offer this kind of love as you serve and grow and lead.

With love,
Amy

Running the Race Well

Dear Jo,

Do you ever look at someone at the pinnacle of their career, excelling at what they do, and feel a thrill? In the movie *Chariots of Fire*, Olympic gold medalist and missionary Eric Liddell famously said, "God made me for a purpose: for China. But he also made me fast, and when I run I feel his pleasure."[1] There is a peculiar joy in doing something in such a way as to know God's pleasure. Few of us will reach the heights of a global gold standard in our fields, but there are milestones to be enjoyed in our chosen career paths.

Paul envisages the Christian life as a race in 1 Corinthians 9:24. In preparing for and running a race, runners need to do certain things. We will run our own race successfully if we practice discipline and form essential habits, alternating between seasons of pressing on and periods of rest and recovery. Putting these elements in place in our fields of service takes a lifetime. So I encourage you to think strategically about each one.

First, you need to spend time developing the habits that will form the backbone of your leadership. These include regular prayer, worship, and Scripture reading. Take part in character-forming discipleship, go on retreats, read books, and go on mission trips. Habit forming also involves the foundational components of your professional career. Earn the needed qualifications, complete apprenticeships, establish a track record of consistent work. The desire to take shortcuts and be propelled into "success" is a particular challenge of our age. Embrace the granular, regular disciplines of your work.

I found this to be profoundly and personally significant while studying for my doctorate at Oxford. I learned to welcome the constructive feedback and insistence on attention to detail. In the hard grind, I found the worth of reaching a standard of work that takes years and is institutionally recognized and verified and for which there are no shortcuts. Learn to love the habits and disciplines needed for your work, and rejoice in the milestones reached by faithful plodding.

Second, during certain seasons, you will need to press on. Do you have the stamina to do so? But also, do you know when to stop pressing on? None of us can live with excessive output and demand all the time. Pressing on loses its meaning if we live in a constant state of overreach. A season of pressing on is characterized by finitude. It entails seeing the finish line of a project or commitment and giving the extra push required to get over it. At times we need to protect our boundaries and well-being, but at other times we need to step up in the moment and press on. The milestones we reach and the achievements we accomplish through moments of perseverance and pressing on often become the foundation stones for our characters and careers.

Third, you need times of rest and recovery. Athletes who prepare for races have days when they do not run or exercise at all. Their muscles are in recovery. Effective leaders learn to exhale, to recuperate, to rest. This might happen over the weekend, on a regular day off, or on vacations or retreats. None of us can work all the time. We need to learn to switch off, go slow, and spend time away from digital devices. Times of rest will not happen unless we prioritize them. I block out time in my calendar in advance so I do not overcommit to work.

The ebb and flow of regular discipline, pressing on, and recuperating is essential for reaching the prize (see Phil. 3:14). Learning when to press on and when to rest is crucial lest we become those who never progress because they fear stretching themselves, or burn out because they never stopped exerting themselves. Healthy flow is possible if we build our leadership on a solid foundation of work, commitment, and rest.

The ebb and flow may be marked in days, but it can also be marked in years. Seasons of life raising young children or years when we need to tend to trauma or mental health may feel like ebbs, but curiously, I have found these seemingly less productive times to be crucial for my development and growth as a leader. Hindsight is a wonderful thing.

We will not always label the seasons correctly, but do take the time to look for periods of habit forming, pressing on, and recuperating. I have found doing so to be invaluable to my growth and development and to help me recalibrate when things have gotten out of balance.

With love,
Amy

Power and Authority

Dear Jo,

Discussions of power dynamics are happening all around us. As you grow in leadership, you will notice that your concern tilts away from how you are treated by others and toward how you are exercising the power you've been granted. Emerging as a person who exercises power after a long period in education, training, and apprenticeship may take you by surprise; it takes some self-reflection to come to terms with the change. Discerning that the power dynamic has shifted is made harder by the fact that typically this change happens over a period of time and may be resisted by people who are threatened by a woman, a young person, and/or a person of color having power. In addition to this, as Christians we are taught to practice humility and submission. This teaching made it harder for me to accept that I did have influence and therefore responsibility to steward it well. Denying the reality of our power is not biblical humility.

The primary model in the New Testament for the exercise of power is ego-emptying service. The Son of Man came not to be served but to serve. Following Jesus means seeking to operate in the power we have with his grace, mercy, and lack of ego. It means raising up others, not seeking fame or acclaim, and using our talents for the sake of his kingdom. In doing this, we should not be paralyzed or downtrodden by others. We exercise power—just not in the way the world does.

One of the greatest hindrances to a healthy acceptance and exercise of the authority God has given is the fear-based methodology "umbrellas of authority." This thinking was popularized by Bill Gothard, the disgraced creator of the Institute in Basic Life Principles, but it lies behind much thinking about power among Christians.[1] Essentially, the argument is that we all need to operate under an umbrella or covering of authority. If we step outside submission to that authority by failing to carry out a command given to us, we bring destruction upon ourselves and anyone under our umbrella. In the family, Christ has the top umbrella, then the husband has his umbrella, and then the wife has her smaller umbrella over the children. The person holding the umbrella is providing a spiritual "covering." Within a church or Christian organization, the male leader has an umbrella above the husband and below Christ. A single woman is under her pastor, leader, or boss, with some believing her father has authority over her until she marries. While many may not openly admit believing this or even realize they have been influenced by it, this thinking lies behind the awkward interactions single women may have within some leadership structures.

This mindset defines leadership by hierarchical expectations of obedience and submission predicated upon fear. The leader operates from the fear that the people underneath them will bring destruction upon themselves if they step out of line. Fear runs up and down the system. This could not be further from a New Testament vision of lavish love for the world that caused the Father to give the Son, or the love that prompted the Son to lay down his life, or the love of neighbor that Jesus calls forth in his followers.

As you think about the power you have, pray about stewardship and servanthood. Resist the fear-based umbrella narrative. If you are tempted to fear that you are stepping out from under man-made umbrellas and that destruction will befall you, or you are afraid that you are not imposing your will strongly enough on those under you, throw away that umbrella. Paul wrote a letter to Timothy, a young leader navigating the challenges of leadership in Ephesus. He said, "For there is one God and one mediator between God and mankind, the man Christ Jesus, who gave himself as a ransom for all people" (1 Tim. 2:5–6). We can't be the mediator for those we lead, and we don't need anyone to be one for us. There is only one mediator between God and us, and it is Jesus Christ.

There is such freedom to be found in letting go of fear and stepping away from hierarchical power dynamics. A Jesus approach to leadership as service, prompted by love, frees us and those we lead from fear. And for us women, stepping up and owning the power we have is godly, honest, and humble if we use that authority to work with truth and integrity, honor the Creator, and serve, love, and empower others.

Don't deny the power or authority you have. Rather, walk in it in a way that reflects Jesus's ego-emptying posture of service and love.

With very much love,
Amy

The Power of Empathy

Dear Jo,

As I reflect on the last two decades of my work and life, one of the things that stands out as most significant in becoming a leader is the power of empathy. Empathy means understanding and even entering into the feelings of others. Being able to see situations and circumstances from the perspective of another person and understand how they are responding and feeling is rarer than you might think. It takes work and imagination to put yourself in the shoes of somebody else, and it requires compassion and attention to engage emotionally. I believe there is also a spiritual dimension to this. The Scriptures use the words *compassion, mercy, service,* and *love* to describe the ministry of Jesus and the characteristics of a disciple.[1] Empathy is needed in evangelism. When we are called to listen to the thoughts and feelings of those seeking or resisting faith, empathy enables us to reach them where they are. Christian apologetics fails at the empathy dimension far more frequently than at the intellectual dimension. Winning arguments is easy; helping a person come to faith is far more difficult.

In leadership, empathy requires that we go beyond techniques or programs that may help people if they follow the steps. Empathy requires us to take on flesh and tabernacle among those we serve. Empathy is incarnational, engaging the whole life of those we lead and disciple, including their emotions, practical challenges, addictions, and personal circumstances.

It is good to ask yourself questions like this: Do the members of my team feel that I care about them? Do my actions, expressions, words, and decisions reflect this? Leading well does not mean pandering to every whim, especially where there is dysfunction. But leading in a way that acknowledges the emotions, likely responses, and preferences of team members will yield positive results.

Over the years, various teams I have either led or been a member of have used tools that purport to achieve better performance from teams. These tools, such as personality tests that box people into "types," have always failed to deliver what they promised, and upon reflection, I think this is because they ultimately dehumanize people. We would do so much better by growing our capacity for empathy, leading with humanity, and living as if those we lead are unique divine image bearers.

The novelist George Eliot believed that empathy was the greatest form of knowledge because it requires us to suspend our human ego and live in another's world. Her novel *Middlemarch, a Study of a Provincial Life* (1857), explores how people can empathize with those they dislike and disagree with. Unlike opinion, empathy requires such levels of self-understanding that we are able to transcend our own likes and dislikes and to see things as another person does. This is not a magical power—it is something we can learn to do. Having strong intuition helps of course, but all of us can cultivate empathy.

There are a few key things you can do to grow in empathy. Start with being curious. Ask questions, and listen to the answers. Resist the tendency to make snap or gut judgments. Cultivating curiosity means you can't be in a hurry. You may feel like you're wasting time, but it's worth it. Read widely, and expose yourself to the opinions of people who are not like you. I listen to more podcasts and news sources from those I disagree with than from people in my culture or with my mindset. Question your own preferences and biases. Having them is healthy as long as you know what they are and don't assume that everyone in your life shares them. Listen to critical feedback. Learn to embrace it. Through my doctoral studies, I learned that the rigorous shredding of my work and ideas made me stronger and more open to others. Use your imagination. Imagine how others feel and think, imagine what it would be like to walk in the shoes of other people, imagine what it might feel like to be on the receiving end of you.

Too many of the mistakes I made or actions I took that hurt people happened when I was in a rush, too busy to stop and reflect and overly confident that my instinct or intuition was absolutely right.

I grew up Anglican. In the liturgy I repeated every Sunday of my childhood, the words just before the confession are based on 1 John 1:8–9: "If we claim to be without sin, we deceive ourselves and the truth is not in us. If we confess our sins, he is faithful and just and will forgive us our sins and purify us from all unrighteousness." We can deceive ourselves. We can live without the truth being in us. What we need is a different perspective and the imagination to see that we may not have everything right. That is the beginning of empathy. Relationship with our Creator offers us this perspective correction through connection to someone outside of us who knows who we are and loves us through it all. The Bible gives us a way to grow and heal—we just need to confess our sin and receive God's forgiveness and cleansing. We learn at the very deepest level of our need for forgiveness through personal experience and weekly exposure to the truth of the Scriptures and the liturgies of the church. Through confession and forgiveness, we build empathy for ourselves and others.

It has been said that empathy is a superpower. In my experience, showing it and being on the receiving end of it certainly make a huge difference in life and leadership, and it is something we can intentionally cultivate.

With love,
Amy

PART 9

Growing Deep Roots

Discipleship as Cultivation

Dear Jo,

I'm writing to you as I look over an orchard on the small con-
servation farm my family and I call home. We care about soil
health, ecosystems, and looking after the natural world. These are
all themes that are relevant to leadership in many settings, even
though they might sound a bit remote to you. In this setting, I have
found myself shaped in my walk with God in creation care by a
particular word: *cultivation*. It speaks to *how* we grow as leaders.
Connection with land and place is a deeply biblical theme. As we
have the responsibility to steward our little piece of earth, God is
speaking to us through the rhythms of the natural world. Have you
ever considered how to connect with the place you find yourself in?

Our farm is small, about seventy acres, and when we took it
on, it had been derelict for twenty years. People talk today about
rewilding, but this land did not need that! One of the orchards
had been untouched by human hands for over sixty years. We had
three acres covered in self-seeded plums, brambles, thorns, and
random trees.

One winter we sensed God saying to us, "I want you to tear it all up and plant an apple orchard." We realized as we looked at that particular piece of land that it was covered in things that were alive and growing, that were taking nutrients from the ground, that were using valuable land—but none of it was producing any fruit. As we looked with spiritual eyes, we thought of the church. The Scriptures remind us that unfruitful growth is not true life.

So my husband and I both took four days off one January and hired a digger. In mud and tears, cold and wind, we cleared three acres, talking and praying as we worked. It was possibly the least restful retreat I have ever experienced. At one point, I said, "I'm not built for manual labor."

Yet halfway through the week I sensed a promise: "Your grandchildren will eat the fruit of these trees." I realized that the same is true with our work. What we plant and grow today in this generation of believers will matter for the generations to come.

That month we planted eighty apple trees in faith.

Cultivation is a major theme in Jesus's teaching. The Christian life is envisaged by Jesus as cultivated—proactively and personally tended by the gardener. And it also unfolds within the challenges of the specific ecosystem and weather around us. No living organism can live in one perpetual season. And the Christian life is not a constant harvest time or perpetual summer. The different seasons entail different kinds of work. Planting, nurturing, fertilizing, taking grafts, replanting things, harvesting, cutting back, moving things around, mulching, and watching as plants lie dormant for a time. In the same way, the various seasons of the soul in our walk with Jesus and our working life will look and feel different, but I have learned that in all of them the tender hand of the gardener is to be welcomed. I want to reassure you that starkly different seasons of your work or life are not something to fear but a sign of health.

Jesus speaks of the Father as the gardener; his hands are at work cultivating us as disciples and working in our communities, the many branches grafted into Jesus himself (see John 15:1).

Jesus speaks of storms that come—weather systems that sweep through, bringing all kinds of apparent destruction. The Father doesn't stop the storms; he cultivates us to be prepared for them. He lovingly tends to us, expecting that the weather and the time we are in will buffet us but that through those experiences we can grow.

Discipleship as cultivation means learning to recognize the times we are in, to make realistic assessments about the impact of the weather systems on us and our communities. It means yielding to the hand of the tender but expert gardener. His pruning is always loving.

The effort to have a perpetual harvest has led to mechanized agriculture that strips the land of nutrients, exhausts the earth with steroid-fueled production and consumption, fights the natural weather systems rather than flowing with them, and leaves people empty from tasteless food and a disorienting disconnection from place. Farmers are often depressed and stressed with bureaucracy.

In much of the church today, we have sought to have mass production religion. Just as agriculture has done, we fight the seasons and look to mass produce a harvest, day in and day out. The more this happens, the more that is needed to produce the same harvest. The very soil is crying out.

The megachurch system in particular has adopted a way of operating that mirrors the mechanized agricultural approach. It has left us weary and disheartened. If you're anything like me, you feel exhausted and jaded by the processes and the promises of numbers-focused churches. If you feel like it's getting harder to see the same amount of fruit with the old methods, perhaps God wants to cultivate rich, new fruitfulness for you. Don't give up on fruit. Don't give up on fruitfulness. But perhaps it is time to lay aside the mechanized system and turn to the loving personal gardener—the Father himself. He makes things grow that are beautiful, that taste good, that produce fruit in season.

I sense a tenderness from God for leaders. He knows the storms that have come: the pandemic, trauma, family worries, bereavement, moral collapses of leaders we admired, and interpersonal meltdowns on teams that leave us weary and hurt. The master gardener knows it all, and he is able to tend to us in our ecosystem—in this time, with this weather.

Let God the gardener do his work of beauty, goodness, and truth in your soul—trust his loving, tender care. Let him prune, and let the storm break off any branches that need to go. Resist the impetus to insist on a perpetual summer, a constant high of the harvest. Welcome the season you are in.

Find ways of getting outside and immersing yourself in the natural beauty of creation. Let God restore your soul in the very place he has called you to live and work. May he cultivate a new fruitfulness as you walk with him.

God is doing something precious even as things are stripped and pruned. He will bring the fruit.

With very much love,
Amy

Wild

Dear Jo,

Last time I wrote to you about cultivation. Today I am walking in the woods at Stampwell Farm, and the bluebells are in bloom. The floor is a carpet of blue, and I feel moved to write to you about the glory of wild things.

There is beauty and fruitfulness in the wild. Take mushrooms. Did you know that far underground there is a web, a kind of communication and nourishment network connecting mushrooms across the land? It is called the mycelial network. But industrial farming machines that dig deep into the earth have broken these chains of connection that put water, carbon, nitrogen, and other nutrients and minerals into the land. Where there is no industrialization, these networks go for miles, and before mechanized agriculture they kept the land fruitful and the soil fertile.

We have so much to learn from the early Christians as we heal from the ravages of greed and the brutality of industrial church methods. In the first centuries of the church, Christians met in homes and spread the gospel through networks of relationships. Missionaries and Christian traders carried the good news of Jesus and established churches, schools, and hospitals all over the world. Hierarchies and political interest came later. The growth of the church was organic and spread like wildfire.

The mycelial network of mushrooms is healing and growing again in Europe. May we leaders say the same of the church across our nations as the wind of the Spirit blows through our weary souls, prepares us to grow, nourishes us with beauty and peace, connects us to others in uncensored freedom, and calls us onward in an invisible, advancing kingdom.

Jesus says in John 3:5–8, 34, "Very truly I tell you, no one can enter the kingdom of God unless they are born of water and the Spirit. Flesh gives birth to flesh, but the Spirit gives birth to spirit. You should not be surprised at my saying, 'You must be born again.' The wind blows wherever it pleases. You hear its sound, but you cannot tell where it comes from or where it is going. So it is with everyone born of the Spirit. . . . The one whom God has sent speaks the words of God, for God gives the Spirit without limit." The Lord gives the Spirit without measure—there is a wildness and an abundance in this promise. When the Spirit comes, the life and abundance that are brought forth exceed the natural.

We are at a moment in the Western church when we need the Lord to come in power upon his church.

The great missionary and theologian Lesslie Newbigin was asked toward the end of his life if he felt optimism or despair over the state of the church. He replied, "I'm neither an optimist nor a pessimist. Jesus Christ is risen from the dead."[1] The resurrection of Jesus makes our schemes and systems irrelevant. The gospel is all about him and his power at work in ordinary people like us.

Wherever we lead in God's kingdom—whether in professional ministry or in other occupations—we have an opportunity to recognize our desperate need of a move of the Spirit and our need for connectedness across cultures and professions. May these relationships and connections spring up for you as you lead. May you find them in unlikely places. May you welcome God's kingdom through networks of grace. Enjoy the wildness of the viral and unsystematic movement of the Spirit. Find God afresh in the wild.

With love,
Amy

Home and Hospitality

Dear Jo,

Today I am writing to you about home. For some people, that primarily means a place—the bricks and mortar of where they live. Before going to university at eighteen, I had lived in seven homes. In the time since graduating, I have lived in another seven places. I write to you from a house I have lived in for twelve years—the longest time I have lived in one house.

Home is a precious thing. It means to be truly and honestly humanly you in a space where you are safe and cherished. A place to be born, to live, and to die with dignity. A thin place where heaven and earth meet. A domestic space where the mundane and the profound coexist. A refuge. Part of growing up is creating a home for yourself and perhaps for others too.

One of the messages to God's people who were in exile in Babylon was "Build houses and settle down; plant gardens and eat what they produce. Marry and have sons and daughters. . . . Also, seek the peace and prosperity of the city to which I have carried you into exile. Pray to the LORD for it, because if it prospers, you too will prosper" (Jer. 29:5–7). An important aspect of life—even life in exile—is creating physical places where life can flourish, where there is beauty and fruitfulness, where there is food and love, gardens and new babies. These things are not unspiritual. The kingdom of God is not a matter of intangible ideas or unattainable asceticism. God's invitation to his people is to build lives and make homes. Some of us leaders work and minister in hard places far from those we know and love. But we still make a place for ourselves and others to live and flourish.

When my husband and I lived in the inner city in a notorious neighborhood in London, we scrubbed and stripped floors, painted walls, and restored windows. We received secondhand furniture. We planted shrubs and fruit trees that future inhabitants would enjoy. He painted amazing pictures, and I served endless meals using my grandmother's plates. We made a home that became a refuge for us and for the many others who stayed or ate there. I often felt unsafe in the seven years we lived there, and we had break-ins. But we prayed and battled and contended for a sense of peace and a feeling of home. We committed to speak life and words of hope over the neighborhood and the house God had called us to live in and to find beauty in the unexpected things. Our first Christmas in that house I bought ornaments for our tree that celebrated London, counteracting the feeling of being hemmed in by the city and its darker elements. I look back on those years as the time when I learned how to make a home. And now when I put those ornaments on the tree every year, I remember and give thanks for that place and all that God did in our time there.

Making a home is worthwhile work that enables something else beautiful—hospitality. To practice hospitality is to share what we have, including our living space, with others. It is interesting to me that this gift is seen in the New Testament as a hallmark of a leader (see, e.g., 1 Peter 4:9; 1 Tim. 3:2; 3 John 1:8).

Hospitality is not always the same as entertaining. When we host a dinner party for friends, we may stray into showing off what we have or our culinary or decorative competence. Hospitality has a spiritual dimension. Abraham hosted angels, and the biblical expectation is that we might experience a similar dynamic when we open our homes. There is a sustenance that is offered and received that connects deeply with the humanity of the people we are serving. Hospitality is an act of generosity—we give our resources of food, time, and love, expecting nothing in return— but it is also an act of vulnerability. We share our safest of spaces with another. We invite others into our home, our refuge, our thin place where heaven and earth connect. We humble ourselves with domestic tasks—cooking, serving, and cleaning.

When my husband and I were first married, we could afford only the smallest of studio apartments in London. It had one room with a separate bathroom. We hosted friends and our church small group weekly in that room. It was such a funny experience packing people into that space. On one occasion we decided to sing a worship song during a Bible study. We had been sitting in a circle, and when everyone stood up, our faces were right up against each other. It was pretty humbling. But it was hospitality. People met Jesus and formed deep friendships in that space.

Over the years, I have realized that one of the ways I can offer hospitality in my home is to cook. It astonishes me how moved people are to receive a home-cooked meal. There is something about the time and love that go into the preparation. The Scriptures speak of a banquet prepared for us by God as a demonstration of his love (Ps. 23:5; Isa. 25:6; Luke 14:15–24). Something happens when we share food prepared with love. It doesn't have to be gourmet. Just learn a few crowd-pleasing recipes, and then learn how to make them for larger numbers—you will be amazed at the impact.

Begin with valuing home, investing in creating a space that is a refuge where your humanity flourishes and where the love of God is felt. From home, hospitality can then blossom. The work and effort are worth it.

With love,
Amy

The Body

Dear Jo,

There is a tremendous emphasis today on the body. Thoughts, ideas, imagination, concepts are receding in importance, while embodied, physical experiences and responses gain in importance. Our own relationship with our bodies can feel strained as we age and change.

What is going on?

One of the predominant worldviews in the West is materialism, that there is nothing other than the physical stuff of the universe. Life is no more than the atoms that make up tangible things, the biochemistry of people, plants, and animals. This belief excludes the possibility of anything spiritual or supernatural. My only life is the embodied, physical life I live here and now. Denying myself a physical or sexual experience is shaming, miserable, and pointless. The only reason to deny self is if it's for my own good, such as keeping my weight down or maintaining health in some way. Religion wants to curtail my freedom pointlessly and deny me the highest and most important transcendent experiences of life. Materialism is closely connected to consumption—the more I consume and experience, the more fulfilled I will be.

Materialism tells me my body is what matters most about me. After all, even my brain is no more than a physical aspect of my body. If I can upgrade or enhance my body, I might be happier. I may want to transition my gender or change my body in some other way. While many people spend lots of time and money upgrading their kitchens or homes, they are now just as likely to spend that time and money on upgrading their face, their body, or their fitness. The body is the zenith of self-realization.

There is a temptation to fall into this way of thinking. But there is also an opportunity here to realize a deep theological truth. The fact that our bodies matter so greatly points to the transcendent source of our lives. As human beings, we were created in bodies to be a reflection of the Creator, who takes on human form at the incarnation. We are made in his image. Our bodies matter. Our value as human beings can truly be known and felt and redeemed through the body of God—which in Jesus Christ was broken on our behalf.

The New Testament describes our bodies as temples that are meant to be indwelt by the Spirit of the living God (1 Cor. 6:19). The longing for bodily meaning and transcendence is accounted for and fulfilled in the Christian faith. Surely, we are not just slime on the face of a great rock, here by chance, a collection of atoms, if our bodies matter in this profound way.

The fact that our bodies matter at a transcendent level is good news for any of us who struggle with our bodies—whether with our weight, our appearance, gender dysphoria, suicidal ideation, chronic pain, limited mobility, or trauma. Our bodies may be a cause for worry, distress, dissatisfaction, or dysfunction. Jesus is good news for any who feel alienated in this world and even within their own bodies. We are invited to encounter him in the sacrament of bread and wine that we eat and drink, to know his presence and redemption not just in theory but in our bones, our flesh, our very bodies.

Your body is a precious gift. You are an image bearer of the Creator. You have been redeemed by the incarnate God in Christ, who suffered for us in this world in bodily form. As you grow in your leadership, you do not have to ignore or silence or punish your body. Your body is a temple in which the Holy Spirit lives. It is right to nurture and pay attention to your body, to take care of it and receive the love of God in it. I am learning how important this is in leadership as I get older. Without falling into a materialistic view in which the body is everything, I can encounter God in my body and live in my body in light of the deep value he places on my whole person, including my body.

With love,
Amy

PART 10

The Value of Stories

Knowing the Storylines

Dear Jo,

I was driving to an event a while ago and mulling over something that had come up the previous year on a call with a friend. She shared how she had been chastising herself for being taken in by a person who had love bombed her and her husband, infiltrating their lives and social network. According to my friend, this person profited through business connections made as a result of the friendship, then slowly but surely turned against her, bringing division in their community and seeking to replace her husband in various leadership contexts.

This person's actions were the cause of tremendous amounts of pain. My friend verbalized how frustrated she felt for not having been more careful—particularly given that this person had left a trail of relational destruction in two previous places of residence. My friend felt humiliated and stupid for having been taken in. She knew about the patterns of suspect behavior to be alert for in theory but had not been able to detect them up close in her own circle.

As I was driving and thinking about what forgiveness means in a situation like this, it struck me that my friend's experience resonated with many stories I knew. What she described could have been a plotline in a novel. I began to reflect on how reading the story right and recognizing the narrative of what is happening can save us from so much anguish.

A few decades ago, a person was not considered "educated" unless they had read the classics, the great novels of literature. Why? On a practical level, once you have read Dickens, you know something of human selfishness and the patterns and stories that create poverty as well as the moral bankruptcy of economically driven men. Reading Tolstoy enables you to recognize the selfish rogue, however romantic, beautiful, and compelling they may seem. Your radar is alert. The great French existentialist novels reveal something of the bleakness of life without God. To be schooled in stories is to know how human beings operate. I realized on that car journey that there were many life situations in which I had failed to recognize the story.

Stories help give meaning to life. No one answers the question "How was your vacation?" with a spreadsheet of data—hours of sunshine, costs of food and drink, statistics about the hotel, the miles walked or swum. We answer with stories. No nation, culture, or family understands its identity in abstract terms—we inhabit the stories of our ancestors and of our people.

Today we are far more likely to watch films than read classic novels, but the stories still matter. Contemporary films contain narrative arcs and recognizable characters. Suspense is built as we anticipate what we think is about to happen. Plotlines emerge. Stories inspire hope and warn us of danger. They lend meaning to our lives and give us patterns to live by.

Stories also matter to God. He chose to reveal himself throughout the Old Testament through an unfolding story. In Christ, God reveals himself to human beings in history as a living, breathing man. The incarnation is enacted, not speculated. Jesus lives a real life that is more story than principle or idea. And stories, often in the form of parables, feature prominently in the teaching of Jesus.

We face various crises of leadership in our cultural moment, but I wonder if one of them is that we have forgotten to look for the story in which we are living. While stories may help diagnose our situations, stories also feed our imaginations and provide texture and intellectual stimulus. They speak to us of what it means to be human and help us find the narrative threads of our own lives.

Ultimately, every Christian lives within a bigger story, one that looks forward to the redemption of all things and a happy ending in a new heaven and new earth. The twists and turns of the narrative along the way are also recognizable, serving as warning, comfort, lament, and encouragement.

As you lead, remember the power of story, and don't lose heart. The end is assured.

With love,
Amy

There Is Hope

Dear Jo,

Today I saw for the first time a photograph of my grandmother (Oma) taken on the day in 1948 when she and her family escaped

Soviet occupation in East Germany and landed in England. In the picture, she is younger than I am today, and she stands with her in-laws and young children at the RAF Northolt station with nothing but the clothes she is wearing.

When my grandfather (Opa), a brilliant scientist, realized that his colleagues were being taken to Siberia to work for the USSR military programs, he made contact with British agents to see if there could be a way out for him and his family. An escape was arranged involving a tiny, unmarked plane landing in a meadow east of Berlin. My father remembers the day well, when the family left their home and everyone they knew and headed out for a walk as if going on a picnic. Tragically, a colleague of my opa who had made a similar arrangement for the following week was shot and killed, along with his entire family.

I grew up hearing the stories of how Oma had met with British agents and passed notes written in invisible ink. At the same time, she was called upon by the occupiers to play music for gatherings of Russian soldiers. She had a rare gift for music. She could hear any piece of music and play it on the piano or accordion. Survival for the family depended on what she called "Beethoven for butter": she would play the piano at concerts for payment in food rations. Her nerves never really recovered.

The photograph I saw today, taken at the moment of their landing in safety, captured the sadness, weariness, and trauma etched onto her young face. She was a refugee. We hear that word all the time now. But today I saw what it meant for one of the women who has most influenced my life. The story of escape, heroism, hope, courage, and liberation had another dimension that struck me afresh: cost. How did a person who endured such strain, fear, and trauma go on to be a source of such light, beauty, laughter, love, and joy in this world? Were people in her generation made of different stuff than we are?

The distress on her face in the photograph reminds me that life brings unexpected shocks. Devastation may well come, but it need not define, embitter, or destroy us. Goodness, beauty, creativity, love, and truth still shine through even in the darkest chapters of life, and they cannot ultimately be taken from us by adversity, betrayal, loss, or war. In middle age, my grandparents had to start over in a new country with nothing. But the fruit of their persistence, love, and work lives on in my life and in the lives of my father, my sister, and my children. We live and flourish because of the choices they made.

As I process shock and upheaval in my leadership due to various losses, I see that I have a living parable in Oma's life. As I think about starting over in a different job and unexpectedly rebuilding work and ministry in midlife, I remember that the kingdom of God prizes the small, the weak, the broken, and the unimpressive as the basis for God's work in this world. Jesus envisaged the kingdom of heaven as being like a mustard seed because it was the smallest seed in common usage in the agriculture of his day. "Though it is the smallest of all seeds, yet when it grows, it is the largest of garden plants and becomes a tree, so that the birds come and perch in its branches" (Matt. 13:32).

Jesus encourages me to think of living, planting, building, and rebuilding that are shaped by his kingdom. Here there is hope, like that of a refugee starting life afresh. The hope is that what we build will matter from generation to generation so that others may come and perch in the shelter of our branches and find safety.

The face of a woman I love captured in a photograph from 1948 reminds me that however dark the trauma or deep the disappointment, there is hope.

With very much love,
Amy

Remember That God Is God

Dear Jo,

Sometimes I need to remember that God is God.

We live surrounded by Christian establishments that talk about God but are essentially secular on a practical level. Systems and protocols are all in place so that the mission, organization, church, or fundraising works without any need for God. The same applies to our individual lives as disciples. We have it all covered. We don't actually expect God to do anything. I know from experience that it is tempting as a leader to use my skills or competencies to work my way into a position in life where I don't need God to be God.

When I was sixteen, I was part of a mission team serving at the Barcelona Olympics and then heading to Morocco. We had a big youth convention in Barcelona with teams that were going out all over Europe to different locations. Our team of forty stayed in a school where we slept on mats on the floor under desks. My friend Abi and I decided to get a couple hours of sleep in the afternoon between events. I fell asleep and had a vivid dream. I saw myself in Afghanistan giving Bibles to the Islamic fighters armed with Kalashnikovs. I told Abi about the dream, and we didn't think much more about it until that evening in the big tent. Floyd McClung was preaching to more than a thousand young people, and in the middle of his message he suddenly stopped and shared, "God is calling somebody here to go to Afghanistan and give Bibles to the fighters there. I'm going to pray for you daily until I sense it is done." I froze. I looked at Abi and stayed completely still. *I hope no one knows it might be me.*

Our trip to Morocco went ahead, and I went back to school. I often thought about the dream and prayed that God would lead me if something was meant to happen.

Years later, during a summer break from my studies at Oxford in 1995, I helped lead a six-week mission trip to China. We spent a day walking and praying on the Great Wall of China, and while we were there we began to pray for the countries to the west of China, all the way to Jerusalem. My friends knew I had an interest in going to Afghanistan someday, and one of them came up and said, "I think I'm meant to go with you." My now husband, who goes by the nickname Frog, felt the same. There on that wall we prayed and decided we would try to go to Afghanistan the following year.

During the course of our second year at Oxford, we made inquiries about getting to Afghanistan. The country was now back in the news because an extreme group called the Taliban had taken over about three-quarters of the country and was ruling with terror. Our friend ran the Oxford University student newspaper, and he agreed to write a letter saying we were the Afghanistan correspondents of the Cherwell Newspaper, on condition that we wrote a piece about our trip. That letter helped us get visas. We booked flights to neighboring Turkmenistan, thinking we would take a train to the border and cross into Afghanistan, as there were no direct flights into the country.

The night before our flight I had another dream. This time I saw the three of us sitting with Taliban leaders and handing out Bibles. On the morning of our flight, on our way to Heathrow Airport, we stopped by the Scripture Gift Mission and collected Bibles and New Testaments in the Afghani languages and some in Russian for post-Soviet Turkmenistan.

My future father-in-law had a friend of a friend who knew the British consul in Turkmenistan, and he agreed to meet us at the airport. His name was Geoff. Geoff took us around in his diplomatic car to hotels he considered safe. We asked for cheaper and cheaper options until he left us at a rather run-down establishment, where we checked in. On every landing, a woman sat at a desk wearing a set of headphones, blatantly listening to what was happening in the rooms of any foreign visitors staying on that floor. There was no attempt to hide this.

My friends and I met to pray and gather our thoughts. As we were looking at a map and trying to figure out our route to Afghanistan, we were startled by the phone in the room. Frog answered and then was silent while the person on the other end spoke. After he hung up, he whispered to us that the woman had said she could rent us a nice, secure apartment. We should get in a taxi and ask for a building called the Circus in the center of Ashkhabad. She had ended the call by saying, "My name is Angela, and I will be wearing a green dress."

When we arrived at the Circus, a woman asked us to get into a car and said she would take us to see the apartment. We climbed into the back of a Soviet-era car, and as we drove away, we looked at each other, wondering if we had done the right thing. She began the conversation by saying, "My name is Angela, and this is our driver. His name is Aslan, which in Turkmen means 'the lion.'" We all felt a wave of relief, having grown up reading Narnia stories. If Aslan was driving, we were going to be okay.

We never found out how Angela came to hear of us or how she had made contact with us. But we were able to plan our trip in safety and seclusion in that apartment. We spent Easter Sunday 1996 worshiping the risen Lord together there.

Remember that God is God.

From there, we caught a train for the seventeen-hour trip to the border of Afghanistan, needing to walk only the final mile to the large metal gates in the middle of the desert. Crossing the border on foot involved walking another half mile or so on a dirt road with land mines on either side and the Bibles burning a hole in our bags.

The Afghan border guards shouted a welcome to us as we arrived and stamped our passports. Then it was time for the dreaded luggage check. We stood and watched as men with guns slung over their shoulders stuck their hands right down into our packs and felt around in them. Each bag contained Bibles with a couple T-shirts on top. The guards did not see the Bibles.

Remember that God is God.

When we arrived in the city of Herat, the only guesthouse still standing let us stay. A journalist from Japan was staying there, bemoaning the fact that the Taliban leadership had just granted their only interview to the BBC. He was leaving the next day. We asked him where he had gone to seek the interview, and he described a café on the rooftop of a building where the Taliban could survey the city and make deals and decisions.

The next day we set out for the café. Every head turned as we walked in, and silence fell. I was the only woman. The Taliban were all visibly armed. We sat at a table and ordered Coke. They served us a locally brewed imitation that tasted faintly of animal fat. Slowly a group gathered around us and began to ask us questions. Thankfully, they had all heard of the University of Oxford. They began to try to convert us to Islam by asking us to repeat the *bismillah*, which we politely refused. When we asked about an interview with the leaders, they told us to return the next day at 3 p.m. There was a slight language mix-up when they told us we were their hostages. When we realized they had confused "guest" with "hostage," our blood pressures returned to healthy levels.

That night my two teammates fell ill—so much so that they were unable to get out of bed. My Bible reading that morning was Psalm 105. In the retelling of the exodus story, the psalm includes the line "Their land teemed with frogs, which went up into the bedrooms of their rulers" (v. 30). Given that my husband's nickname is Frog—it seemed relevant. We prayed for healing, and the three of us set out for the café at the appointed time.

Remember that God is God.

Eventually, the man who had arranged the interview for us arrived at the café and drove us to the Taliban military headquarters on the outskirts of town. When we got out of the car, the education minister, who had been sent to greet us since he spoke English, looked at me in shock. They hadn't realized a woman would be coming. UNICEF had just pulled out of the region because the Taliban had refused to meet with its female leader. A woman was not allowed in their presence. Frog said, "She must stay with us, as we fear for her safety." I knew I would not be able to speak, so I took the role of notetaker and Bible carrier.

We were led up some stairs and through layers of security to the central room of the house. The room had mattresses around the outside walls. The education minister told us the leaders slept there, as it was the safest and most closely guarded room in the house. Distant gunfire could be heard. In the room, we met the foreign minister, the keeper of the Holy Quran (the religion minister), and some others.

After hours of interview and sharing of food, our team began to speak of Christ. One said, "We have brought you a gift—we believe this is the most precious gift one person can give another." Then another added, "It is the Holy Bible." I got out the Bibles, and we handed them over. The religion minister spoke, and the education minister translated. He said, "I know exactly what this book is. I have prayed to Allah for years that I could read this. Thank you for bringing this book. I will read it every day until I finish it." Everybody visibly relaxed. The education minister asked if he could have a Bible in English. He wanted to read and practice his English. He returned in the car with us to the guesthouse to collect an English Bible.

Remember that God is God.

For the next day or so, we walked the streets and gave out New Testaments in the homes and shops we were invited into. Many people invited us in and asked in hushed tones for a book. There was a palpable hunger for God's Word.

I learned in those few days, unlike at any other time in my life, that God is God. He surpasses our understanding, capacities, abilities, and faith levels. God is God, and that changes everything.

Have you domesticated God? Have you put God into a manageable religious box? Let's not live our lives functioning as Christian atheists who have a framework of cultural belief but no space or room or need for God to show up as God. As leaders, even in our competence and plenty, let's remember that God is God. In our suffering, struggle, and grief, let's remember that God is God. Let's wait on him, love him, be surrendered to him. This is the most important thing I can share with you. Live your life in light of this one truth: God is God.

With love,
Amy

Afterword

The final letter of this collection speaks of one of the most formative experiences of my life. As Christians in the twenty-first century, living in the West, we can believe in the existence of God and accept the evidence that Jesus of Nazareth was God incarnate, that he was crucified for our sins and rose from the dead three days later. However, we live our lives without the expectation of direct intervention by God, and we build our ministries, churches, and communities using systems and processes that eliminate the need for God to provide, show up, change situations, or miraculously intervene. The faith the New Testament describes is very far from this. Connection with the living God is known, felt, experienced, persuasive to others, and demonstrably real. God is God. That means he transcends our ideas, abilities, categories, and expectations. He is the Creator, the source of all life, our redeemer, our liberator, and the one who pours love into our hearts by the Holy Spirit. He is also Lord—an authority above our autonomy, preferences, and failures. He is our comforter and provider. He forgives, restores, and empowers those who turn to him.

Any leadership that operates as if God is not God, whatever our theoretical belief system, will ultimately falter. Yet the more competent we become, the greater the temptation to operate within a system that does not need God to be God. As you grow and learn and your opportunities and influence increase, keep your relationship with God at the center of your life and expect God to be God. Invite him to show up as God. Teach those you lead how to know and encounter the living God. Expect him to surprise you and to surpass your categories and past experiences. Life with God is an adventure. Don't miss out on the fullness of the journey.

Acknowledgments

Writing a book is a labor of love, and this one has been especially exacting given the personal nature of the letters. Thank you to my nearest and dearest, my husband, Frog, for your loving support, words of encouragement, and patience with my worries and workload. Thank you for believing in me far more than I ever have. You are the most wonderful, creative, joy-filled, and uplifting person I know. To my sons, Zac, JJ, and Benji, words can't express how much I love and admire each of you. I pray that you will continue to grow in leadership and life with integrity, excellence, and compassion.

Thank you to my agent, Joy Eggerich Reed. You have supported me and this project with extraordinary commitment, encouragement, insight, and care. Thank you to Katelyn Beaty, my editor at Brazos, for your editorial genius and the sheer excellence with which you conduct yourself. Thank you, Rio Summers, for your support of this book from its earliest inception as individual letters and all your creative genius.

Thank you to my dear friends Nancy Gifford, Julia Manning, Julia Sloan, Julie Wanstall, Sarah Yardley, Abi Willetts, Jo Saxton,

Chris Caine, and Beth Redman. I admire and love you all and have learned so much from each of you as a leader. Thank you to my community of leaders at Latimer Minster. Spending early Sunday mornings with you is unfailingly inspiring and challenging. Thank you to the many Christian leaders who have invited me to work alongside you at conferences, churches, businesses, and universities. I have learned so much more from you than I have offered. Thank you to all the colaborers advocating for victims of injustice and abuse in public and behind the scenes. You give me hope.

And lastly, to the women this book is written for, the rising generation that is pressing forward and taking up positions of leadership, may you know the blessing, peace, and goodness of the one you serve. And may you hear the encouragement of those of us a few years on. We are cheering you on and ready to support you as much as we can.

Notes

Letter 1 Proclamation

1. D. Martyn Lloyd-Jones, *Preaching and Preachers* (London: Hodder & Stoughton, 1971), 97.

2. This is from one of Dietrich Bonhoeffer's Finkenwalde Lectures on Homiletics, published in Clyde Fant, *Bonhoeffer: Worldly Preaching* (New York: Thomas Nelson, 1975), 101.

3. Ben Witherington III, *The Acts of the Apostles: A Socio-Rhetorical Commentary* (Grand Rapids: Eerdmans, 1998), 17.

Letter 2 Speaking in Public

1. Elizabeth Blankespoor, Bradley E. Hendricks, and Gregory S. Miller, "Perceptions and Price: Evidence from CEO Presentations at IPO Roadshows," *Journal of Accounting Research* 55, no. 2 (2017): 275–327.

Letter 3 Owning Our Embodied Voices

1. Maria S. Tsantani, Pascal Belin, Helena M. Paterson, and Phil McAleer, "Low Vocal Preference Drives First Impressions Irrespective of Context in Male Voices but Not in Female Voices," *Perception* 45, no. 8 (2016): 946–63, https://journals.sagepub.com/doi/full/10.1177/0301006616643675.

Letter 4 Don't Hold Back

1. Saira Moazzam et al., "Gender Differences in Question-Asking at the 2019 American Society of Hematology Annual Meeting," *Blood Advances* 4, no. 21 (2020): 5473–79, https://www.ncbi.nlm.nih.gov/pmc/articles/PMC7656936.

Letter 5 Calling Unfolds

1. As it turned out, a particular professor had taken issue with something I had argued and insisted on this course of action to publicly address it.

Letter 6 God Calls Work Good

1. See Dorothy L. Sayers, *Why Work?* (London: Metheun & Co, 1942).
2. Sayers, *Why Work?*, 12.

Letter 8 Becoming Lovers of Truth

1. Dorothy L. Sayers, "Gaudy Night," essay in *Titles to Fame*, ed. Denys Kilham Roberts (London: Nelson and Sons, 1937), 82.
2. Dorothy L. Sayers, "What Is Right with Oxford?," *Oxford* 2, no. 1 (1935): 36–37.

Letter 13 How to Read 1 Timothy 2

1. Kenneth E. Bailey, "Women in the New Testament: A Middle Eastern Cultural View," *Theology Matters* 6, no. 1 (January/February 2000): 8.
2. Bailey, "Women in the New Testament," 9.
3. John Chrysostom, "Homilies on First Timothy," New Advent, accessed October 10, 2023, http://www.newadvent.org/fathers/230609.htm.

Letter 14 Learn to Say Yes!

1. Christine L. Exley and Judd B. Kessler, "The Gender Gap in Self-Promotion," *Quarterly Journal of Economics* 137, no. 3 (2022): 1345–81.

Letter 15 Who Gets the Credit?

1. Juliet Eilperin, "How a White House Women's Office Strategy Went Viral," *Washington Post*, October 25, 2016, https://www.washingtonpost.com/news/powerpost/wp/2016/10/25/how-a-white-house-womens-office-strategy-went-viral/.

Letter 18 My Experience in an Abuse Crisis

1. Daniel Silliman, "Ravi Zacharias's Ministry Investigates Claims of Sexual Misconduct at Spas," *Christianity Today*, September 29, 2020, https://www.christianitytoday.com/news/2020/september/ravi-zacharias-sexual-harassment-rzim-spa-massage-investiga.html.

2. Lynsey M. Barron and William P. Eiselstein, "Report of Independent Investigations into Sexual Misconduct of Ravi Zacharias," Miller & Martin PLLC, February 9, 2021, https://www.courthousenews.com/wp-content/uploads/2021/02/zacharias-report.pdf.

Letter 19 When Institutions Cover Up Abuse

1. Jennifer J. Freyd, "What Is a Betrayal Trauma? What Is Betrayal Trauma Theory?," Center for Institutional Courage, accessed December 12, 2023, http://pages.uoregon.edu/dynamic/jjf/defineBT.html.

2. Jennifer J. Freyd, "What Is DARVO?," Center for Institutional Courage, accessed December 12, 2023, https://pages.uoregon.edu/dynamic/jjf/defineDARVO.html.

Letter 22 Gaslighting

1. The movie *Gaslight* was released in 1944 by Metro-Goldwyn-Mayer.

Letter 26 Trauma

1. Dr. Gabor Maté makes this observation in the trailer for the film *The Wisdom of Trauma*, which can be viewed at https://drgabormate.com/the-wisdom-of-trauma/.

2. Here are just a sampling of the resources available on post-traumatic growth after trauma: Arielle Schwartz, *The Post-Traumatic Growth Guidebook: Practical Mind-Body Tools to Heal Trauma, Foster Resilience, and Awaken Your Potential* (Eau Claire, WI: PESI Publishing & Media, 2020); M. Rutter, "Resilience Concepts and Findings: Implications for Family Therapy," *Journal of Family Therapy* 21 (1999): 119–44; Richard G. Tedeschi and Lawrence G. Calhoun, *Trauma and Transformation: Growth in the Aftermath of Suffering* (Thousand Oaks, CA: Sage, 1995).

Letter 27 When You Can't Pray

1. "A Collect for Aid against Perils," in *The Church of England Book of Common Prayer* (1928).

Letter 29 Reframing Forgiveness

1. Desmond Tutu, foreword to *Truth and Reconciliation Commission of South Africa Report*, vol. 1, Truth and Reconciliation Commission, October 1998, https://www.justice.gov.za/trc/report/finalreport/volume%201.pdf.

2. Queen Elizabeth II, "Christmas Broadcast of 2016," December 25, 2016, https://www.royal.uk/christmas-broadcast-2016.

3. Desmond Tutu, foreword to *Truth and Reconciliation Commission of South Africa Report*, vol. 6, Truth and Reconciliation Commission, March 2003, https://www.justice.gov.za/trc/report/finalreport/vol6.pdf.

Letter 34 Running the Race Well

1. *Chariots of Fire*, directed by Hugh Hudson, written by Colin Welland (Los Angeles: Twentieth Century Fox, 1981).

Letter 35 Power and Authority

1. Bill Gothard, *Research in Basic Principles of Life: Advanced Seminar Textbook* (Hinsdale, IL: Institute in Basic Life Principles, 1986).

Letter 36 The Power of Empathy

1. On compassion, see Luke 6:36; on mercy, see Matt. 5:7; on service, see John 13:15; and on love, see Luke 6:27.

Letter 38 Wild

1. As quoted in Tish Harrison Warren, "The American Church Is a Mess. But I'm Still Hopeful," *Christianity Today*, June 15, 2021, https://www.christianity today.com/ct/2021/june-web-only/church-decline-attendance-still-hopeful.html.

AMY ORR-EWING (DPhil, Oxford University) is an international speaker, theologian, and apologist. She is the author of multiple books, including *Mary's Voice*, *Where Is God in All the Suffering?*, and *Why Trust the Bible?* Orr-Ewing speaks at churches and on university campuses around the world and has spoken in the UK Parliament, the US Capitol, and the West Wing of the White House. She previously served as president of the Oxford Centre for Christian Apologetics and is an honorary lecturer at the University of Aberdeen. She lives near Oxford, England, with her husband and their three sons.

CONNECT WITH AMY:

website: www.amyorr-ewing.com

 amyorrewing.online

 @amyorrewing